AQA

A LEVEL MUSIC

Revision Guide

First published 2017 in Great Britain by
Rhinegold Education
14-15 Berners Street
London W1T 3LJ, UK
www.rhinegoldeducation.co.uk

You should always check the current
requirements of your examination,
since these may change.

Editor: Katharine Allenby
Cover and book design: Fresh Lemon Australia

AQA A Level Music Revision Guide
Order no. RHG143
ISBN 978-1-78558-158-8

Exclusive Distributors:
Music Sales Ltd
Distribution Centre, Newmarket Road
Bury St Edmunds, Suffolk IP33 3YB, UK

Printed in the EU

AQA

A LEVEL MUSIC

Revision Guide

RICHARD BRISTOW &
RICHARD KNIGHT

RHINEGOLD
EDUCATION

Contents

The authors

Richard Bristow

studied Music at Jesus College, Oxford, before completing his PGCE at the University of Southampton. Richard is currently Director of Music in a highly-successful independent school in London where he oversees the music curriculum and the extensive co-curricular programme.

He also has significant experience as a senior examiner at A Level, specialising in composition, as well as working for Keynote Education to deliver student conferences and teacher courses across the UK. Richard is active as both a performer and a composer; the BBC Singers have recorded his setting of the 'Agnus Dei' and he can regularly be found singing with various choirs in London and the South.

Richard Knight

read Music at St John's College, Oxford, and has been Director of Music at two leading independent schools. He also has nearly 20 years' experience as a senior examiner at A level and is also an examiner for the ABRSM in the UK and overseas.

Richard is a prolific composer with a large catalogue to his name including opera, orchestral, chamber and instrumental works (see www.rokmusic.org.uk). His works have been performed at the Tête à Tête Opera Festival in London and in various recitals in the UK and elsewhere. Some of his Christmas church music has been performed by the Ex Cathedra and Tenebrae choirs, and his *Preludes for Piano* are being recorded by the pianist Naomi Kayayan in 2018. Richard also conducts the Malvern Festival Chorus. He has a particular interest in all things South American.

Introduction

The fact that you have picked up this Revision Guide must mean your A Level examination is getting close.

Here you will find some useful reminders:

- How the paper structured
- How many marks each section is worth
- Which Area of Study is relevant to each section

All being well you will feel confident that you have covered all the topics and set works required. There is plenty more information and detail about these in the Rhinegold Education *AQA AS and A Level Study Guide.*

In the exam room what is being tested is your understanding of music. The test is partly aural – the music you are given to listen to – and partly knowledge-based – the vocabulary and technical explanations of what the musical terms mean.

Of course, in the exam you are on your own; working through this book by yourself in advance is a good way to check how confident you are about the knowledge required. There are exercises to check yourself, and prompts to start and organise your revision process.

In the end no author or teacher can put the knowledge into your head unaided – that is down to you. Give the revision process your full focus, uninterrupted by distractions, and be determined to keep at it until you know that you know it, and your understanding is complete.

About Unit 1: Appraising Music

Unit 1: Appraising Music is the written examination of the AQA A Level Music qualification.

The examination lasts for 2 hours 30 minutes and is divided into three sections relating to different musical skills and Areas of Study (AoS):

Section A: Listening

- Answer *all* questions on AoS1: Western Classical tradition 1650–1910

  Three strands of study:

  - The Baroque solo concerto
  - The operas of Mozart
  - The piano music of Chopin, Brahms and Grieg

- Answer *all* questions on **two** other AoS (2–7 from the list below)

Section B: Analysis

- Answer **two** questions from a choice of three relating to the three strands in AoS1

Section C: Essay

Answer **one** essay from **one** AoS from 2–7. There is only one question for each AoS.

Using this revision guide

This book is divided into different chapters, each relating to a different AoS. For the A Level examination, you must study AoS1 and two other AoS from the following:

- AoS2: Pop music
- AoS3: Music for media
- AoS4: Music for theatre
- AoS5: Jazz
- AoS6: Contemporary traditional music
- AoS7: Art music since 1910

AoS1 requires you to learn lots of specific musical vocabulary, much of which also features in AoS2–7. It is important that you work through this first chapter, developing your understanding of the different strands and completing the exercises to aid your knowledge.

The chapters that follow are set up to aid your general musicality, develop your listening skills, and revise the specific musical concepts inherent in each of the AoS. While you could only look at the chapters relating to your chosen AoS, it would be more beneficial to work through each of the chapters, allowing your vocabulary and musical understanding to expand. The listening questions in each chapter might use the named artists for that specific AoS but are often based on similar concepts, allowing you to develop your listening skills and gain all-important examination practice. Relish the chance to expand your musical horizons!

There is a glossary beginning on page 147 which contains many of the musical terms you will need to know for this exam.

Western Classical tradition 1650-1910

Introduction

AoS1 is different to the remaining AoS in a number of important ways:

- It is **compulsory**
- The musical elements vocabulary for this AoS can also be tested in questions relating to other AoS
- Listening questions will involve an aural dictation question (Q.2)
- It involves the study of specified set works
- You have to answer **two** Section B questions based on the set works
- You do <u>not</u> write an essay on AoS1 music in Section C

The AQA A Level Music specification can be found at www.aqa.org. uk/subjects/music/as-and-a-level/music-7272. This contains a full list of the relevant vocabulary for each AoS. Further examples and explanations can be found in the *AQA AS and A Level Music Study Guide* (Rhinegold Education).

Strands and set works

There are three strands to this AoS at A Level:

- Baroque: the solo concerto
- Classical: the operas of Mozart
- Romantic: the piano music of Chopin, Brahms and Grieg

In Section A, the listening questions will be based on music that belongs to these strands, but will **not** use music from your set works.

The listening questions will be structured as follows:

Q1	An extract from one of the strands with short answer questions	4 marks
Q2	An aural dictation question based on music from another of the strands	6 marks
Q3	A long answer question based on the remaining strand	10 marks

The set works you will have studied are:

Baroque solo concerto:

- Purcell: Sonata for trumpet and strings in D major Z.850 – all three movements
- Vivaldi: Flute Concerto in D major Op. 10 No. 3 'Il Gardellino' RV 428 – all three movements
- Bach: Violin Concerto in A minor BWV1041 – all three movements

The operas of Mozart:

- The Marriage of Figaro (*Le Nozze di Figaro*) K.492, Act I

  The following numbers only:

  - Overture
  - No. 1 Duettino (Figaro and Susanna, including following recitative)
  - No. 3 Cavatina (Figaro, including the previous recitative)
  - No. 4 Aria (Bartolo)
  - No. 5 Duettino (Susanna and Marcellina)
  - No. 6 Aria (Cherubino)
  - No. 7 Terzetto (Susanna, Basilio, Count)
  - No. 9 Aria (Figaro)

Romantic piano music

- Chopin: Ballade No. 2 in F major Op. 38
- Chopin: Nocturne in E minor Op. 72 No. 1
- Brahms: Intermezzo in A major Op. 118 No. 2
- Brahms: Ballade in G minor Op. 118 No. 3
- Grieg: Norwegian March Op. 54 No. 2
- Grieg: *Notturno* Op. 54 No. 4

Musical language for this Area of Study

An important part of your revision in this Area of Study should be the technical vocabulary listed in the specification.

All the terms found here can also be tested in your optional Areas of Study, so they should be a priority for your revision.

The following exercises should enable you to check your understanding of these important words by looking at short musical examples. In Section A of the Appraising Music paper you have to be able to do this in response to the *sound* and not the score, so it is recommended that while doing these exercises by looking at the music given, you also play the tunes and listen to how they sound while thinking of the relevant vocabulary.

Meanwhile, this method of revising the terms – by seeing examples of each term in notation – should directly help you to prepare for the analysis questions in Section B of the Appraising Music paper.

Melody words

Exercise 1 – Contours

Study the following melody and fill in the bar numbers that match the descriptions of the melodic **contour** in the chart underneath:

Description	Bar number(s)
An ascending scalic contour	
A descending scalic contour	
An ascending arpeggio contour	

A descending arpeggio contour	
A triadic contour	
A conjunct (non-scalic) contour	
A disjunct contour	

Exercise 2 – Special melodic notes

Consider the following piece and describe the function of the notes specified in the chart below it by using the appropriate words from the following list:

- **Passing notes** – accented, unaccented, chromatic
- **Auxiliary notes** – upper, lower, chromatic
- **Appoggiatura**
- **Note of anticipation**
- **Echappée note**

Position (bar/beat)	Note name	Description
1²	C	
1³	A	
4¹	A	
4²	F	
5¹	C♯	
6¹	A	
7¹	F♯	
11³	D	
12¹	A	
12³	B♭	

Exercise 3 – Intervals

Using the previous piece (see Exercise 2) identify the following intervals in the melodic line:

Bar	Notes	Interval
2	D – G	
3	D – B♭	
3-4	F – A	
11	E♭ – C	
11	F – E♭	
13	E♭ – A	

Exercise 4 – Melodic devices

The vocabulary for this exercise includes:

- **Motif**
- **Sequence** – rising and falling
- **Fragmentation**
- **Inversion**
- **Intervallic augmentation** and **diminution**

Study the melody of the piece below and then answer the questions that follow.

Questions about the melodic line (tick each correct answer):

1. **Bars 1–10 comprise:**

   six phrases of imbalanced lengths ☐

   two balanced 5-bar phrases ☐

   one long phrase of 10 bars ☐

2. **The first four notes are best described as:**

   Theme ☐

   Phrase ☐

   Motif ☐

3. **The A♯ in bar 2 is...**

   A chromatic passing note ☐

   A lower chromatic auxiliary note ☐

   A chromatic appoggiatura ☐

4. **Compare bars 6²–7¹ with bars 1²–2¹. The technique used is:**

   Repetition ☐

   Sequence ☐

   Intervallic augmentation ☐

5. **Compare bars 14–16 with bars 11–13. The technique used is:**

   Repetition ☐

   Rising sequence ☐

   Falling sequence ☐

6. **Compare bars 17²–18¹ with bars 1²–2¹. The technique used is:**

   Fragmentation and inversion ☐

   Fragmentation and sequence ☐

   Intervallic diminution and inversion ☐

7. **In bars 19-20 the technique used is:**

Fragmentation ☐

Repetition ☐

Rising sequence ☐

8. **The melodic contour in bar 24 is best described as:**

Disjunct ☐

Triadic ☐

Arpeggio ☐

9. **The sequence in bars 25-28 is:**

Falling by step ☐

Falling by a 3rd ☐

Falling by a 4th ☐

10. **In bars 30-33 the technique used is:**

Sequence ☐

Fragmentation ☐

Repetition ☐

Exercise 5 – Ornamentation

Complete the table below by naming each of the ornaments given and assigning them the correct notation for how they are played, choosing from A-F in the following examples.

Ornament symbol	Ornament name	How played: give letter name to show which example above is the written-out form of this ornament
A		
B		
C		
D		
E		
F		

Harmony words

Exercise 6 – Diatonic chords and inversions

The diatonic chords are usually labelled using Roman numerals (I–VII) with 'b' added for 1st inversions and 'c' for 2nd inversions. V^7d is the 3rd inversion of the dominant 7th (with the 7th in the bass). It is often the custom to use capital Roman numerals for chords which are major, and lower case for chords which are minor (with italics sometimes used for diminished chords).

Here are the chords of C major and A minor:

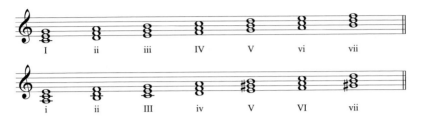

Identify the chords of the following piece in B♭ major by putting Roman numerals underneath each one.

Exercise 7 – Cadences

You need to be familiar with the following cadences:

Perfect	V to I	including the common approach via Ic (a cadential 6/4)
Plagal	IV to I	also known as the 'Amen cadence'
Interrupted	V to a surprise	often vi (other options include I♭7b or a diminished 7th)
Imperfect	various to V	including Ic to V (known as a half-close), and ivb to V (known as a phrygian cadence)

Now consider the music below and fill in the chart for each of the cadences in the piece.

Bar	Key	Chords	Cadence
2			
4			
6			
8			
10			
12			
14			
16			
18			
20	G major	V – I	Perfect (NB 4-3 suspension on V)

Exercise 8 – Advanced chords

In addition to diatonic chords, you need to be familiar with handling and analysing the following more advanced harmonic options:

- Diminished 7ths
- Secondary dominant 7ths
- Substitution chords (e.g. iv in a major key)
- Chord of the Neapolitan
- Augmented 6th chords (Italian, German and French)
- Tierce de Picardie

Study the following music and then analyse the chords listed in the chart underneath:

Chord	Chord analysis
Bar 3²	
Bar 5¹	
Bar 5²	
Bar 7²	
Bar 9²	
Bar 11	

Bar 13²	
Bar 18	
Bar 19¹	
Bar 22	

Exercise 9 – Keys: signatures and relationships

By this stage your understanding of the tonal system should be strong. Test yourself with this quiz:

1. How many sharps are in B major?

2. How many flats are in A♭ flat major?

3. What is the relative minor of E♭ major?

4. What is the relative major of F♯ minor?

5. When a piece in F minor modulates to its dominant, to which key does it change?

6. Which major key has 4 sharps?

7. Which minor key has 5 flats?

8. When a piece in B minor modulates to its subdominant, to which key does it change?

9. What key is the enharmonic equivalent of D♯ minor?

10. If a piece in B major modulates to the enharmonic equivalent of its median major, to which key does it change?

Texture words

It can be tempting to think that the answer to every texture question is a single word ending in -phony. This is not a helpful instinct to have.

There are three aspects to texture:

- How many notes are used at any given point?
- In what context or role do each of these notes belong?
- In which registers do the notes occur?

The possible contexts or roles include: melody, doubling of melody at a 3rd (or other interval), countermelody, imitative contrapuntal line, bass line, pedal note, accompaniment figuration, inner part to chord, and so on.

Only when you have considered these angles should you reach for a texture label word; sometimes it is best to describe a texture without using a -*phony* word.

Test yourself on the definition of these terms by filling in the table:

Texture term	Definition
Monophonic	
Unison	
Octaves texture	
Parallel 3rds	
Melody and accompaniment	
Homophonic	
Polyphonic	
Contrapuntal	
Fugal	
Canonic	
Antiphonal	

Tempo, metre and rhythm words

What you need to know:

- Italian terms for tempo: (from slow to fast) grave, adagio, lento, largo, larghetto, andante, moderato, allegretto, allegro, vivace, presto, prestissimo
- Terms that cause tempo to change: ritenuto, rallentando, rubato, accelerando
- The difference between simple time (the beat subdivides into two, such as $\frac{2}{4}$, $\frac{3}{4}$, $\frac{4}{4}$) and compound time (the beat subdivides into three, such as $\frac{6}{8}$ and others, giving two main beats in a bar)

Dynamics and articulation words

What you need to know:

- The normal Italian abbreviations for dynamics from *pp* to *ff*, and also *sfz* and *fp*
- The signs and sounds of different standard types of articulation: accent, legato, marcato, staccato, and tenuto (see the glossary at the back of the book)

Sonority and timbre words

What you need to know:

- The names and sounds of all standard orchestral instruments and vocal types. You may need to hear the difference between a viola and a cello, an oboe and a bassoon, or a soprano and a mezzo-soprano
- The name and sound of special techniques that are applicable to these instruments. For example:
  - Strings: pizzicato, arco, sul tasto, sul ponticello, col legno, con sordino, double stopping
  - Singing: Sotto voce, portamento and vibrato

Structure words

What you need to know:

You need to understand what is meant by the following terms:

- Binary form
- Rounded binary form
- Ternary form
- Ritornello and episode
- Recitative
- Aria
- Sonata form
- Through-composed

See the glossary at the back of the book for any terms you are unsure about.

Remember: you are now a specialist music student and should be using this vocabulary like it is your mother tongue!

Practice for Section A questions on AoS1

Preparing for question 1

Question 1 will be based on an extract of music from one of the three strands, and requires short answers. The questions could be about any element of music (melody, rhythm, harmony, texture, structure, and so on).

There follows an extended question on each of the three strands that covers many of the types of question that the examiners might set. Remember that, in the actual exam, the question will be based on a shorter excerpt of music, which you can listen to as often as you need. The exam question will be worth 4 marks.

QUESTION 1 – BAROQUE

Preparation

Due to the style and genre of music being set, likely questions include:

- Identifying the solo instrument
- Understanding whether the passage is a ritornello or solo passage
- Commenting on the basso continuo (if present)
- Spotting harmonic progressions such as rising sequences of circle of 5ths patterns
- Identifying modulations

Of course, the best way to prepare for a question 1 on this strand is to listen frequently (actively, with your mind focused on the music) to a wide range of different concertos from the period. Good composers to explore include Corelli, Vivaldi, Handel, Torelli, Locatelli, and Bach. Try listening to concertos for as many different solo instruments as you can find (such as violin, viola d'amore, cello, flute, oboe, bassoon, trumpet, harpsichord, organ, and mandolin).

This question uses Vivaldi's Concerto RV495, first movement, which can be found at: http://bit.ly/VivaldiRV495

Extract required is: 0:45–2:45

You will hear the start of a solo concerto by Vivaldi. The music is in $\frac{3}{8}$ time, and the home key is G minor.

1. The movement begins with a tutti section. What is the opening interval in the melodic line? Underline your answer.

   Perfect 4th   **Perfect 5th**   **Octave**   **Perfect 12th**

2. What is the texture of the string instruments in the opening section?

3. What is the tonality of the music in the opening section?

4. Which of the following is heard in the opening tutti section?

   Circle of 5ths harmony   **Neapolitan 6th**

   Rising sequence   **Tonic pedal**

5. What is the solo instrument?

6. There are three main subsections to the first solo passage.
   Which of the following is an accurate description? (Tick your answer):

   a. A passage over a descending bass played twice
      A passage based on a rising harmonic sequence
      A passage over a descending bass with slower
      harmonic rhythm   ☐

   b. A passage over a descending bass played twice
      A passage based on circle of 5ths harmony
      A passage over a descending bass with faster
      harmonic rhythm   ☐

   c. A passage over a descending bass played twice
      A passage based on circle of 5ths harmony
      A passage over a descending bass with slower
      harmonic rhythm   ☐

   d. A passage over a descending bass played twice
      A passage based on a rising harmonic sequence
      A passage over a descending bass with faster
      harmonic rhythm   ☐

7. In which key does the second ritornello start?

8. To which key does the second ritornello change after two short phrases, and then finish?

9. Early in the second solo section there is a rising sequence. How many bars long is the phrase that is used for this sequence? Underline your answer.

   1 bar   **2 bars**   **3 bars**   **4 bars**

10. Name the harmonic device that Vivaldi uses for the central portion of the second solo section.

11. In what key is a shortened ritornello heard after the second solo section? Underline your answer.

   Relative major   **Relative of the subdominant**

   Relative of the dominant   **Tonic major**

12. The final solo passage heard also starts with a sequence. Which of the following is an accurate description of this solo? Tick your answer.

   a. A rising shape treated to rising sequence

   b. A passage over a descending bass played twice

   c. A falling shape treated to rising sequence

   d. A falling shape treated to falling sequence

QUESTION 1 – CLASSICAL

Preparation

- Identifying the voice type (soprano, bass, and so on)
- Spotting what type of movement is being heard (recitative, aria, and so on)
- Commenting on the vocal line (range, intervals, ornaments, and so on)
- Hearing how the singer is accompanied – texture and instrumentation
- Analysing cadences

Of course, the best way to prepare for a question 1 on this strand is to listen frequently (and actively, with your mind focused on the music) to items from Mozart's many operas. Best of all, try to get to a performance of one of them – a night out at the theatre! In addition to the opera that provides your set work movements – *The Marriage of Figaro* – other famous operas by Mozart include *Idomeneo*, *Così fan tutte* and *The Magic Flute*.

This question uses an aria from *The Magic Flute* called 'O Isis und Osiris' sung by Sarastro, the High Priest of the Sun. The German words and a translation are as follows:

SARASTRO:

1. O Isis und Osiris, schenket   O Isis and Osiris, give

2. Der Weisheit Geist dem neuen Paar!   The spirit of wisdom to the new pair.

3. Die ihr der Wand'rer Schritte lenket,   She who links to her the wanderer's steps,

4. Stärkt mit Geduld sie in Gefahr,   Strengthens them with patience in danger,

5. Stärkt mit Geduld sie in Gefahr.   Strengthens them with patience in danger.

CHORUS:

6. Stärkt mit Geduld sie in Gefahr.   Strengthens them with patience in danger.

SARASTRO:

7. Lasst sie der Prüfung Früchte sehen;   Let them see the fruits of the test;

8. Doch sollten sie zu Grabe gehen,   But, if they should go to the grave,

9. So lohnt der Tugend kühnen Lauf,   Then, the valiant course of virtue rewarded,

10. Nehmt sie in euren Wohnsitz auf,   Receive them in your abode,

11. Nehmt sie in euren Wohnsitz auf,   Receive them in your abode.

CHORUS:

12. Nehmt sie in euren Wohnsitz auf,   Receive them in your abode.

The music can be found at: http://bit.ly/MozartIsisOsiris

1. What voice type is the singer? Underline your answer.

    Countertenor   Tenor   Baritone   **Bass**

2. What is the metre of the music?

3. What is the most appropriate tempo marking for the music? Underline your answer.

    Adagio   Andante   Allegretto   Moderato

4. On which degree of the scale does the vocal line begin? Underline your answer.

Tonic   **Mediant**   **Dominant**   **Leading note**

5. Which word best describes of the vocal contour for line 2? Underline your answer.

Arpeggio   **Disjunct**   **Scalic**   **Triadic**

6. Identify the interval of the rising leap on 'Schritte' in line 3. Underline your answer.

Major 6th   **Minor 7th**   **Major 7th**   **Octave**

7. What cadence occurs on 'in Gefahr' at the end of line 5? Underline your answer.

Ic – V^7 – I   **Ic – V^7 – VI**   **ii7b – V^7 – I**   **ii7b – V^7 – VI**

8. Identify the choral texture in line 6. Underline your answer.

Antiphonal   **Octaves**   **Homophony**   **Polyphony**

9. What chord underpins 'Prüfung Früchte' in line 7? Underline your answer.

Augmented 6th   **Diminished 7th**

Neapolitan 6th   **Secondary 7th**

10. In which two lines of text does the singer have the same line as the bass of the orchestra?

11. Which combination of wind instruments is playing in the orchestra? Tick your answer.

a. Oboes, Clarinets and Horns ☐

b. Oboes, Bassoons and Horns ☐

c. Clarinets, Bassoons and Trombones ☐

d. Trumpets, Clarinets and Bassoons ☐

12. Which of the following is the correct description of the key scheme of this aria? Tick your answer.

a. The music modulates to the dominant halfway through and stays there to the end ☐

b. The music modulates to the relative minor and returns to the tonic in the second half ☐

c. The music modulates to the relative minor and then ends in the dominant ☐

d. The music modulates to the dominant halfway through and returns to the tonic in the second half ☐

QUESTION 1 - ROMANTIC

Preparation

Due to the style and genre of music being set, likely questions include:

- Melodic contours and phrase structure, including sequence and inversion
- Chord identification
- Modulation and cadences
- Textures and pianistic sonorities
- Ways in which the music is expressive

Of course, the best way to prepare for a question 1 on this strand is to listen frequently (i.e. with mind focused on the music) to a wide range of piano music by the three composers of the set works. Piano music by other 19th century composers such as Mendelssohn, Schumann and Tchaikovsky can provide relevant additional experience. Best of all, if you are a pianist, learn to play some of the music yourself.

Among the pieces you might look at are:

- Chopin: Mazurkas Op. 30 (or others)
- Brahms: Waltzes Op. 39
- Grieg: Albumblätter Op. 28

This question uses Brahms's Waltz in A♭ major Op. 39 No. 15. The music can be found here: http://bit.ly/BrahmsWaltz

1. The piece comprises six phrases – two different phrases repeated a number of times. What is the structure? Tick your answer.

   a. A A B A A B ☐

   b. A A B A B A ☐

   c. A B A A A B ☐

   d. A B A A B A ☐

2. The music is in $\frac{3}{4}$ time. How many bars long is:

   a. The 'A' phrase? _____

   b. The 'B' phrase? _____

3. What is the rhythm of the opening two bars of melody in each phrase? Write the rhythm on the line below:

4. In the opening two bars of the 'A' phrase, the melody is doubled in the pianist's right hand at which interval? Underline your answer.

   3rd   4th   6th   Octave

5. The 'A' phrase begins on chord I. On what chord does the 'B' phrase begin? Underline your answer.

   I   IV   V   V⁷

6. What harmonic device is used in the opening four bars?

7. What is the chord on the downbeat of bar 3 in the 'A' phrase? Underline your answer.

   I   IVc   V⁷   vib

8. What chord is played in bars 5–6 of the 'A' section? Underline your answer.

   Ii   iii   IV   vi

9. With which cadence does the 'A' section end? Underline your answer.

   Imperfect cadence in I   Imperfect cadence in V

   Perfect cadence in iii   Perfect cadence in vi

10. Which of the following devices is used in the 'B' phrase? Underline you answer.

Circle of 5ths harmony   **Inversion**

Pedal note   **Rising sequence**

11. What chord is heard in the penultimate bar of the 'B' phrase? Underline your answer.

Augmented 6th   **Diminished 7th**

Neapolitan   **Secondary dominant 7th**

12. What new note value is used as a decoration in the final phrase? Underline your answer.

Minim   **Triplet crotchet**   **Triplet quaver**   **Semiquaver**

Preparing for question 2

Question 2 tests your ability to notate the music you hear, a skill called 'aural dictation'. This is a very useful ability to have; like so many musical talents, it takes practice – you can't really 'revise' it the week before an exam. You should try to do some every day. You can try writing down ringtones, sirens, theme tunes, tunes you are learning to play (without looking at the music!), and so on.

QUESTION 2

Here are three useful challenges:

1. Write down the tune for the British national anthem. The first two bars have been given for you:

2. Write down the tune for 'Happy Birthday'. The first two bars have been given for you:

3. Remember that some of the notes you are asked to notate for aural dictation in the exam might be bass line notes and in the bass clef. Practise this by listening to the famous 'Air' from Bach's Orchestra Suite No. 3 in D major and writing out the bass (cello) part for the first half of the piece. Focus on the following aspects in order to help you:

- The octave leaps

- The sense of descending scale

- Any sense of sequence in the bass line

- Where chromatic notes occur

The first four notes and the last one are written in for you:

QUESTION 3

Question 3 will ask you to identify stylistically typical features of an extract from the strand from AoS1 that has not been examined so far in Section A.

Depending on the strand, the focus of the question will vary.

When question 3 is set on Baroque Concerto, the focus could be:

- Ritornello form

- Virtuosity of the solo instrumental part

- The style of the individual composer (Purcell, Vivaldi or Bach)

When question 3 is set on Mozart opera, the focus could be:

- The structure
- The sense of Classical style
- Ways in which the personality and intentions of the character are portrayed

When question 3 is set on Romantic piano music, the focus could be:

- The structure
- The characteristics of the type of piece (e.g. Nocturne)
- The style of the individual composer (Chopin, Brahms or Grieg)

There are 10 marks available on this question.

It is very important that you answer this question referring in detail to the piece of music you have chosen to write about. The examiners are **not** asking 'What are the typical features of a Baroque concerto/Mozart's operas/ Romantic piano music?' You need to listen carefully to identify specific aspects of the music they have set for your exam paper.

You are advised to spend 25 minutes on questions 1–3, and 10 of the 20 marks are for this question, so you should take time to consider all the different angles: melody, rhythm, harmony and tonality, texture, instrumentation and structure.

Among the aspects you might listen out for are:

Baroque concerto

Melody	Texture	Instrumentation
A ritornello with a strong head motif	Unison strings in the ripieno	Use of basso continuo
Solo passagework based on triadic patterns	Polarised texture of soloist and bass line	Harpsichord and/ or lute
Trills and mordents	Active bass line	**Structure**
Harmony	**Rhythm**	Contrast between tutti and solo passages
Rising sequences	Long runs of semiquavers	Fragmentation of the ritornello to provide accompanying motifs
Circle of 5ths progression (with 7ths maybe)	Anacrusis	
Use of suspensions	Dotted patterns	

pairing phrases

Mozart opera

Melody

Antecedent and consequent phrases

Periodic phrasing

Scalic and triadic contours

Trills and turns

Appoggiaturas and accented passing notes

Harmony

Heavy reliance on I and V

Significant structural cadences using cadential 6/4

Texture

Simple bass line

Use of delicate accompaniment figures

Rhythm

Answering phrases having the same rhythm

Possible use of triplets

Instrumentation

Presence of a woodwind section in the orchestra – maybe including clarinets

Horns used to blend orchestra together

Structure

Possible use of Recitative

Significant use of modulation to V

Romantic piano music

Melody

Range of melody

Asymmetric phrase structures

Use of sequence

Appoggiaturas

Fioritura

Harmony

Diminished 7ths

Secondary dominant 7ths

Neapolitan

Augmented 6ths

Substitution chords

Enharmonic keys

Texture

Melody and accompaniment

Tenor and bass register melodies

Rhythm

Hemiola

Cross-rhythms (e.g. duplets v triplets)

Instrumentation and Sonority

Sustaining pedal

Una corda

not the same

Practice for Section B questions

Section B is based upon your study of the set works. There are **three** questions, and you have to answer only **two** of them:

- Question 22: Baroque solo concerto
- Question 23: Mozart opera
- Question 24: Romantic piano music

In each case a single, substantial passage of music will be the basis of the question. This will be provided both as an audio track and in score form on the question paper.

There are 17 marks available: 2 of these are for short answer questions identifying specific analytical details. Then there is a 5-mark question which will ask you to consider the extract from the angle of one of the constituent elements (such as melody or rhythm) linking this to the wider context of the piece and/or composer. The other 10 marks are for a long answer addressing the whole excerpt and discussing how its musical details combine to create the musical whole.

It is recommended that you spend 20 minutes answering each of the questions you choose to answer.

SAMPLE QUESTION 22

Use your favourite recording of Vivaldi's Concerto 'Il Gardellino' in conjunction with this score and the question beneath.

1. What is the interval between the last note of bar 5 and the first
   note of bar 6 in the 1st violin?   **[1 mark]**

2. What is the name of the harmonic progression used in bars 5–8?   **[1 mark]**

3. Discuss Vivaldi's use of the ripieno instruments, highlighting
   the different ways he uses them across the extract.   **[5 marks]**

4. Discuss the composer's handling of melody, tonality and texture
   in the extract, showing how he creates structure from these
   elements. In your answer you should make reference to
   specific details in the score.   **[10 marks]**

   [Total: 17 marks]

SAMPLE QUESTION 23

Use your favourite recording of the opening duettino from *The Marriage of Figaro*, in conjunction with this score and the question beneath.

1. What term best describes Susanna's melodic contour in
   bars 17³–18³?   [1 mark]

2. What falling interval does Figaro sing in bar 28?   [1 mark]

3. Discuss how Mozart uses his orchestra to reflect the dramatic
   situation on stage.   [5 marks]

4. Comment on melody, harmony and tonality, and rhythm, and
   show how Mozart uses the conventions of a sonata form exposition
   in this passage of music to portray his two characters. In your answer
   you should make reference to specific details in the score.   [10 marks]

[Total: 17 marks]

SAMPLE QUESTION 24

**Use your favourite recording of Grieg's *Notturno* in conjunction with
this score and question beneath.**

1. What kind of triad is used at bar 2 beat 2?   [1 mark]

2. What melodic device is used in the phrase structure for
   bars 5–8?   [1 mark]

3. Discuss how Grieg uses rhythm and metre to create
   a sophisticated musical effect   [5 marks]

4. How do harmony and texture combine to generate a
   nocturnal atmosphere in this piano miniature?   [10 marks]

[Total: 17 marks]

Revising the set works

General advice

The movements that AQA have chosen as set works will contain the passages that are set in Section B of your written paper. Therefore, the better you know these pieces,

- the more fluently you will be able to work in the 40 minutes you spend answering the two questions you have chosen

- the more you will be able to write accurate analytical detail (rather than general overview commentary)

- the more marks you will get!

So how do you get to know these set movements? There are a number of ways; some will seem obvious, others perhaps less so:

- Listening to recorded performances of the music

- Listening to recorded performances while following the score

- Reading the score silently, without listening to the music (like reading a novel)

- Playing/singing the music – maybe you play the instrument(s) intended by the composers, maybe your school orchestra can tackle one of the pieces, however....

- ...one of the best ways is to make your own arrangement of the music for you and your friends to play: maybe as a piano duet, in a wind quintet, a brass group, a 'Swingle Singers' style vocal group, or a rock band

Ultimately, if you want the best understanding you can gain, you need to approach the pieces in as many guises as you can: listener, analyst, performer, arranger, and so on. This way your brain will make connections between all these experiences; these connections will be *your* understanding of the music.

There is a lot of analytical detail in the *AS and A level Music Study Guide* (Rhinegold Education). Over the next few pages is a series of prompts for each of the set pieces – angles which you ought to think about when you are revising these pieces.

Remember: ultimately the examiners are looking for evidence of your understanding of the music; this is far more important than trying to memorise lots of information that someone else has written and which is only based on *their* understanding.

Baroque solo concerto

Purcell: Sonata for trumpet and strings in D major Z.850

General points to consider:

- The significance of the harmonic series to the 17th century trumpet
- The lack of valves limiting the notes available to the trumpeter
- Purcell's interest in unusual harmonic twists
- The piece pre-dates the popularity of ritornello form

First movement:

- Melodic contours that use quaver rests, pairs of semiquavers, leaps of 4ths and 5ths, trills
- Textures that include simple detached chords, a partial fugal dimension, antiphony between trumpet and strings, string activity under an inverted pedal on the trumpet
- Unusual passages of harmonic writing
- Contrast between sections created by subtle changes of rhythm/note value

Second movement:

- How contrast is created with the previous movement through instrumentation, tonality and texture
- Purcell's interest in chromatic harmony and the open 5th at bar 4^3

Third movement:

- The gigue-like character generated by the rhythmic profile
- The use of hemiola at cadences (for example in bars 80–81)
- The extent to which the texture is contrapuntal/fugal
- The skilful blend of conjunct melodic contour and large leaps, and the use of melodic inversion at bar 82

Vivaldi: Flute concerto in D major Op. 10 No. 3 'Il Gardellino' RV428

General points to consider:

- Vivaldi's prolific writing of concertos
- The programmatic element of suggesting birdsong in the melodic writing

First movement:

- Ritornello form: the main sections (tutti/solo) and key centres
- The melodic contour of the ritornello theme and its constituent ideas

- Use of circle of 5ths harmonic patterns and rising sequences
- The virtuosity of the flute part, its bird-like aspects, its interplay with the violins in the ripieno
- The variety of the bass line throughout the movement, including the octaves texture of the ritornello, long pedal notes in the cello, and passages where the violas provide a 'walking' bass line
- The role of the basso continuo

Second movement:

- Binary form, modulating to the dominant at the halfway point
- Flute accompanied by basso continuo only: effectively chamber music
- Rhythmic influence of the Siciliano
- The use of sequence in the second half, initially visiting E minor before returning to the tonic

Third movement:

- Another ritornello movement visiting the dominant and the relative minor
- The main theme using a descending scale and repeating tonic-dominant patterns
- Lots of trills and oscillating semiquavers in the solo flute and 1st violins
- The use of dotted quaver and semiquaver in the solo flute
- A significant dominant pedal

Bach: Violin Concerto in A minor BWV1041

First movement:

- Ritornello form: the main sections and key centres
- The importance of the initial anacrusis with its rising 4th which pervades so much of the music
- The intricacies of the melodic line with its rhythmic drive (anacruses, tied notes, flowing semiquavers) and harmonically focused contour (including sequences)
- The active bass line with scales, auxiliary notes and moments of strong angularity (for example leaps of a diminished 7th)
- Complexities of harmonic progressions – not just circle of 5ths but the use of Neapolitan chords from bar 135
- Changes of harmonic rhythm

Second movement:

- A riff-like cello/bass line provides the focus of the ritornello
- Use of the violas as the bass line in solo passages (compare with Vivaldi, 'Il Gardellino' first movement, bar 32)
- The beauty of the solo line using a mix of long and short note values, ties and trills, and triadic and conjunct motion
- Changes of tonal centre
- Distinctive harmonic colours (for example, bars 13–14 and 17)

Third movement:

- The Gigue-inspired ritornello that – in true Bach fashion – is also fugal!
- The I – V: V – I harmonic basis to the start of the solo, but with long lower appoggiaturas in the second and fourth bars
- Use of circle of 5ths harmonic progressions (for example, from bar 33)
- Use of bariolage from bar 105

Mozart opera: *The Marriage of Figaro*, Act 1 (selected numbers)

General points:

- The use of twinned phrases, tonic-dominant harmony and articulating cadences
- The influence of sonata form as an element of the style of the music – especially modulating to the dominant for a secondary theme/idea
- Melodies that use scalic and triadic shapes
- Mozart's skill at using the musical vernacular of his day to portray a range of human personalities and motivations

Overture:

- The initial flowing, conjunct idea for strings centred on the tonic and moving to the dominant above and below
- A more homophonic idea for winds, related to notes of the harmonic series, then culminating in the first tutti to complete the first subject
- The contrasting second subject – playful with long chromatic lower auxiliary notes (D♯s) – and skittish woodwind writing in parallel 3rds
- Some enriching chromatic harmony later in the second subject (often suggesting minor keys)
- A codetta of classic Classical credentials
- The absence of development: instead, after 16 bars to convert an A major chord from being the tonic (at the end of the exposition) to being the dominant, the music heads straight into the recapitulation

No. 1 Duettino:

- The use of sonata form principles with the first subject representing Figaro and the second subject representing Susanna. He ends up singing her tune!
- Parallel contrasts of melodic contour, syllabic/non-syllabic word-setting, and instrumentation in the accompaniment
- The variety of textures between the two vocal parts
- Reasons why the recapitulation is shorter than the exposition

No. 3 Cavatina:

- The unusual ABCA structure
- The influence of the Menuet on the music: 4-bar phrases, diatonic harmony, simple rhythms
- The use and significance of the horns
- The more elaborate texture and harmonic palette of the B section in response to the text
- The additional dimension of characterisation in the C section

No. 4 Aria:

- The use of sonata exposition in bars 1–50
- The portrayal of Bartolo's assertive character through a disjunct melody of wide register
- Aspects of the music that convey rage including: running semiquavers, staccato wind chords, harmonic adventure including an augmented 6th chord in bars 46–48
- A free-flowing middle section with a long line of triplet quavers to test the singer

No. 5 Duettino:

- The juxtaposition of elegant melody and restless triplets in the orchestra
- The relationship of the two singers' vocal lines

No. 6 Aria:

- The ternary form of the opening section (bars 1–51)
- The ways in which the first section conveys impetuousness through rhythm, intervallic augmentation, quickening harmonic rhythm and placement of the top note in the melodic contour
- Use of chromaticism and appoggiaturas to suggest sighing
- The instrumentation including the clarinets
- Mozart's skill in the second half of the aria in creating a thrilling ending to a 'show-stopper' number

No. 7 Terzetto:

- Skilful characterisation of the three contrasting personalities
- Count Almaviva: short, blunt melodic lines with dotted rhythms, diatonic
- Don Basilio: conjunct falling phrases, chromatic twists in the accompaniment avoiding strong cadences
- Susanna: emotional intensity achieved through chromatic upper auxiliary in first entry, use of diminished 7th in bar 35

No. 9 Aria:

- Rondo structure
- Simple tonic-dominant harmony predominates
- A mix of militaristic elements (dotted rhythms, triads) and playful, pretty aspects (turns, light textures)

The piano music of Chopin, Brahms and Grieg

Chopin: Nocturne

- The skilful way harmony is woven into the LH triplet figuration which also includes upper appoggiaturas on the fifth note of the six-note pattern
- Abridged sonata form structure
- Asymmetric phrase structure
- Duplet quavers in the RH against the triplet rhythms in the LH
- Advanced chromatic harmony including diminished 7ths (for example, bars 5 and 7), augmented 6ths (bar 6) and Neapolitan with its own dominant 7th (bars 14–15)
- The use of pedal notes in the B sections

Chopin: Ballade

- The ABABA structure
- Alternating F major and A minor (relative of the dominant) tonal centres
- Largely diatonic, mid-register A sections
- Chromatic Presto B sections exploring wide registers and varied textures; dominated by semiquavers

Brahms: Intermezzo

- A ternary design using both F♯ minor (the relative of the main tonic – A major) and F♯ major for the wistful middle section
- The use of expressive leaps in the melodic contour
- The avoidance (mostly) of root position chords in the opening passage
- Rhythmic displacement of the sense of downbeat from bar 16^3 and other cross-rhythms including hemiola and duplets against triplets

Brahms: Ballade

- A ternary structure (ABA) in which the 'A' section is itself in ternary form
- The significant of the ratio of three quarters to one quarter – either as dotted minim + crotchet, or dotted crotchet + quaver
- The use of phrases of five bars in the Aa sections and six bars in the Ab sections
- The tertiary key relationship to the B section

Grieg: March

- The use of syncopation within compound time to create folk feel
- Use of the 'Grieg motif' and sequences in the melodic writing
- Sonorities enhanced by the use of open 5ths (possibly violin- or bell-inspired?)
- The use of non-diatonic triads within a secure C major context

Grieg: *Notturno*

- Ternary form + coda
- Sumptuous chromatic harmony in the main section using many half-diminished 7th chords and the Neapolitan of the dominant
- Further harmonic sophistication in the B section using chord extensions including 9ths and 11ths
- A final cadence of IIIb – I (the mediant used as a surrogate dominant)

Pop music

Introduction

This is an exciting, contemporary and probably familiar Area of Study looking at pop music and the development of the genre.

There are six named artists in this AoS for you to listen to, study, and gain a critical appreciation of. You should seek to establish *how* they create their particular sound world by detailed analytical study of their music.

For the purpose of this specification, pop music is defined as popular mainstream music derived from and including a number of musical genres, including rock, funk and R&B, from 1960 to the present.

- Stevie Wonder
- Joni Mitchell
- Muse
- Beyoncé
- Daft Punk
- Labrinth

This chapter will look at accessing the key vocabulary listed in the AQA specification, with some sample listening questions similar to Section A and a sample essay for Section C of the written paper.

The AQA A Level Music specification can be found at www.aqa.org. uk/subjects/music/as-and-a-level/music-7272. This contains a full list of the relevant vocabulary for each AoS. Further examples and explanations can be found in the *AQA AS and A Level Music Study Guide* (Rhinegold Education).

Musical language for this Area of Study

In addition to a full working knowledge of the vocabulary listed for AoS1, AoS2 also requires you to be familiar with specific vocabulary found in the music of the named artists.

The following approach can be used for the pieces you have studied to ensure you are familiar with these musical concepts. The answers can be found at the back of the book.

Harmonic analysis

Chord symbols are an essential part of this AoS and having a good working knowledge of chord symbols, advanced chords and chromatic chords will greatly help your understanding. Complete the following exercise, writing out the chord in staff notation.

A good way of approaching this is to:

1. Establish the major or minor triad

2. Observe whether the bass is in root or inversion

3. Establish whether the chord is extended – for example 7th, 9th, 11th, 13th – or diminished (º) or augmented (⁺)

4. Establish if there is a suspension (for example sus4), pedal point, or additional added notes

G⁷/B   C   C⁷/E   D   C♯dim   Dsus4   B⁷/D♯   Em

Use of studio/technological effects

Many pieces in this AoS are processed using advanced music technology software. It is vital that you understand and can hear these processes.

- **Chorus**: two individual sounds with similar timbral qualities and pitch placed together to sound as one. 'Timbral' relates to the timbre of a sound, which is its particular quality or tone colour

- **Delay**: a controlled echo which is repeated at a specified time, often getting quieter with each repetition

- **Reverb**: electronically-produced echo
- **Distortion**: often used on electric guitars by increasing the gain, giving a different timbre
- **Panning**: using the left and right parts of the stereo field

STUDY PIECE 1

Stevie Wonder, 'Higher Ground'

You can find this song here: http://bit.ly/StevieWonderHigherGround

One approach to understanding the various vocabulary terms listed in the specification is to hear them in action. Using a table like the one below is one way of identifying the concepts and giving an aural example of where they are used in the piece.

		Intro	Verse	Chorus
Tonality	Blues Scale	X		
	Pentatonic			
	Mode use			
Harmony	Pedal Point			
	Chord Symbols	X		
	Complex chords			
	Chord Extensions	X		
	Sus4 chords			
	Power Chords			

Melody	Blue Notes	X
	Glissando/Slide	
	Hook	X
	Syllabic	
	Melisma	
	Pitch Bend	X
	Riff/Ostinato	X

Having listened to the introduction you may have noticed the following:

- The opening one bar riff/ostinato using a rising profile (E♭–G♭–A♭) in the bass. This acts as a memorable one bar hook

- The use of G♭ – use of blues scale

- Use of flattened 7ths (D♭s) on the tonic E♭ chord, creating an extended chord of E♭⁷

- Use of triplets complete with pitch bends between the notes

Completing your aural analysis

Now complete the table for the verse and chorus which follow, adding a cross for each feature you hear in the music. Having done this, write a short bullet point to give greater musical analysis to your point, as in the example above. You may wish to add this to your own musical glossary for the elements, listing where you can hear them.

> By creating your own musical glossary, similar to the one at the back of this revision guide, you will be able to cross reference quickly where musical devices occur, allowing for more effective revision.

STUDY PIECE 2

Muse, 'Mercy'

You can find this song here: http://bit.ly/MuseMercy2015

Listen to the song and answer the following questions as an introduction to the piece:

1. How many chords are used in the introduction?

2. The opening is diatonic in the key of G major, with only one chromatic note appearing. Where does this note occur? How is this note related to the tonic?

3. What is the interval sung on the word 'change'?

Completing an aural analysis in this way can help you to access a piece initially, before you go on to create a more complete musical analysis.

Task

Listen to the whole song. Write four questions on the piece for one of your peers to answer, using the example questions above as a guide. Remember to include the answers separately, citing examples where possible. As your peers answer your questions you can answer theirs.

> Peer-to-peer working is a great way to revise the information needed for your exam.

Listening (Section A)

Track 1 – Joni Mitchell, 'Blue'

Listen to this song, which you can find here: http://bit.ly/BlueJoniMitchell

Extract: 0:00–0:45

1. What note values are used by the right hand of the piano in the opening four-bar introduction? Underline your answer:

   Minims   Crotchets   Quavers   Semiquavers   [1 mark]

2. What is the harmonic rhythm of the introduction?   [1 mark]

3. What melodic device is used when the voice first sings the word 'blue'?   [1 mark]

4. What is the range of the melody in the extract *'songs are like tattoos you know I've been to sea before'*? Underline your answer:

   7th   Octave   9th   10th   [1 mark]

   [Total: 4 marks]

Track 2 – Daft Punk, 'Instant Crush'

Listen to this song, which you can find here: http://bit.ly/InstantCrushDaftPunk

Extract: 0:00–0:46

1. The excerpt is based on a repeated four-chord sequence. Which line is the correct sequence?

   a. G♭ E♭m B♭m A♭   ☐

   b. G♭ B♭ A♭m D♭   ☐

   c. G♭ E♭m B♭m D♭   ☐

   d. G♭ A♭m D♭ A♭   ☐   [1 mark]

2. Which **one** of the rhythm patterns below is used as an ostinato in this extract?

a. ☐

b. ☐

c. ☐

d. ☐ [1 mark]

3. Describe how the text is set in the opening four-bar verse.   [2 marks]

[Total: 4 marks]

Question 1 can be worked out on a basic level by establishing the order of major and minor chords in the extract. This narrows down the possible correct answers.

Track 3 – Beyoncé, 'Ave Maria'

Listen to this song, which you can find here: http://bit.ly/AveMariaBeyonce

Extract: 0:00–2:06

This excerpt is taken from a song called 'Ave Maria' which translates as 'Hymn to the Virgin'.

Explain how the musical elements are used to convey the religious nature of this title.   [10 marks]

[Total for AoS2 Section A: 18 marks]

Essay question (Section C)

In the examination, you have to answer one essay question. There will be only one set for each AoS, so there is no choice beyond which AoS you have studied. You have 45 minutes to write the essay which is marked out of 30.

The full mark scheme can be viewed on the AQA website. This shows in detail the mark band breakdown for the essay question.

Remember to plan your essay fully before embarking on writing it.

At A Level the essay question is likely to ask you to compare the music of up to three different named artists in your response.

Task – Essay Analysis

1. Read the sample essay below, look online at the mark scheme, and mark it yourself, considering:

   - The accuracy of musical vocabulary and detail
   - The use of supportive musical examples with detailed analysis
   - Whether the writing shows an aural awareness of the piece
   - The accuracy of spelling, grammar and written communication to give a mature writing style
   - Whether the essay answers the question fully

2. Compare your marks and thoughts with your peers to form a class discussion. How did your teacher mark the essay? Compare this to the marked copy in the answers section at the back of the book.

3. How can this candidate improve their mark? Write a teacher-style comment for the essay, including a target for improvement.

4. Now write the essay yourself, taking these ideas into consideration.

'The key to writing a great pop song is to write a memorable riff.'
To what extent do you agree? Discuss with reference to at least *two*
pieces by *two* different named artists.

Named Artist 1: Stevie Wonder 'Superstition' (1972)

Named Artist 2: Labrinth 'Beneath your beautiful' (2012),
'Let the Sun Shine' (2010)

'Superstition' by Stevie Wonder is a famous funk-inspired piece with
an opening bass riff which is iconic. The key characteristics of funk
include a complex groove, interjections from the horn section and
interlocking drum patterns and many of these features can be
found in the piece. It uses the Eb minor pentatonic scale with four
straight quavers followed by a more complex second part of the bar.
The second clavinet part plays an Eb major 7 chord underneath this
two-bar riff, giving an Eb(b7#9) chord with the major and minor
3rd played simultaneously. The bass guitar anchors the riff, playing
on the beat Ebs before increased quaver movement in the final two
beats of the bar. Wonder's vocals also employ the Ebm pentatonic
scale with subtle syncopation over this accompaniment, dovetailing
with the three-layered texture.

While the riff itself is memorable and central to the song, it is by no
means the only factor in the success of the piece. The piece develops
in three main ways. Firstly, Wonder introduces a horn riff (tenor
saxophone and trumpet) at 'thirteen month old baby'. This new
riff has an ascending profile using semiquavers, again employing
the pentatonic scale, peaking on a top Bb. The use of ties aids the
syncopation. A second development occurs in the short chorus, where
the harmonic rhythm changes to two chords per bar, outlining V7, bvi7
and V7 secondary dominant (V7b of V) in minims before settling on
IV7 for a whole bar, eventually resolving to a crotchet V+ augmented
triad on Bb. This chromatic chord allows for a one-bar breakdown

to interrupt the flow of the music. Finally, a four-bar link with the horn section prominently using C natural in a contrasting descending pattern leads into the bridge which repeats the chorus chords complete with a vocal 'howl'. This allows the music to achieve a sense of repetition and change, sustaining musical character.

Many successful pop songs do not make use of memorable riff patterns, with Labrinth's 'Beneath Your Beautiful' being one such song. The four-bar introduction uses repeated constant quavers in the piano right hand with an ascending two-bar pattern in the left. The chords are anchored on D (the tonic) and A (the dominant) though there is some gentle dissonance to help give the ballad feeling – for example, the G major 7 chord in bar 2. The verse is reliant on a repeating two-bar chord sequence of D Em G A with the piano playing block chords, allowing the vocals (complete with gentle syncopation) to have the musical focus. Interestingly, the chorus (from 'would you let me') uses the same chord pattern as the verse with a few small developments, including adding a 7th to the Em chord, 9th to the G major chord and at the line 'take it off now' adding a new B minor chord. Later in the song Emeli Sandé joins Labrinth's vocals, with both singing in 3rds to develop the musical texture. The song ends with a repetition of the opening.

'Let the Sun Shine', another Labrinth single released in 2010, is another successful song which makes use of a riff in a different way. Here, the rhythmic groove is relaxed with a tempo of crotchet = 110 which is animated by use of a semiquaver riff played on one high note on a synthesizer. This figure uses semiquaver rests (on the 4th, 9th and 16th semiquaver beats) as well as one quaver on the 11/12th beats to add musical excitement to the song. However, the riff is not the main musical focus here with the vocals having dominance. The chord progression, like in 'Beneath your Beautiful' is a simple repetitive cycle of Em C and G, with the bridge having greater harmonic venture including a flatwise modulation to Eb, Cm7, F and Bb. The bass, using dotted rhythms, is also simple in construction, being used from the first chorus onwards. It is the combination of these elements which allows for the success of the song, not the riff alone.

While the use of riff remains an important part of pop song composition, it is by no means the only aspect required to create a successful piece of pop music. Popular music which gains fame makes use of a combination of elements – memorable melodic lines, pleasing chord progressions, development of ideas and use of riff – to create a piece which is musically satisfying.

AoS2 KEY TERMS: A SUMMARY

Melody: riff, pitch bend, melisma, syllabic, hook, slide, glissando, ostinato, blue notes

Harmony/Tonality: power chords, sus4 chords, chord extensions/symbols, complex chords, tonic and dominant pedal, modes, pentatonic, blues scale

Structure: Intro/outro, middle 8, bridge, breakdown, verse, chorus, instrumental, break, drum fill, fade in/fade out

Timbre: studio effects, instruments and use, vocal timbres, instrumental techniques/effects

Texture: looping, layering, a cappella

Tempo, metre and rhythm: bpm, metronome mark, groove, backbeat, irregular metre

Music for media

Introduction

Music for media is a wonderfully exciting Area of Study that looks at the intricate relationship between music and action.

There are five named artists in this AoS for you to listen to, study and gain a critical appreciation of. Through detailed study of their music, you should seek to discover how their music confirms, suggests, questions and ultimately supports the unfolding drama.

This AoS looks at music especially composed for film, television and gaming, from 1958 to the present.

- Bernard Herrmann
- Hans Zimmer
- Michael Giacchino
- Thomas Newman
- Nobuo Uematsu

You are encouraged to answer the questions in this revision guide to aid your listening skills and learn more about essay technique. Some of the key vocabulary for this AoS is duplicated in other AoS; check your knowledge and develop your understanding by completing the exercises presented in the chapters on these other AoS, developing your musical ear.

The AQA A Level Music specification can be found at www.aqa.org. uk/subjects/music/as-and-a-level/music-7272. This contains a full list of the relevant vocabulary for each AoS. Further examples and explanations can be found in the *AQA AS and A Level Music Study Guide* (Rhinegold Education).

Musical language for this Area of Study

Timbre and Sonority

Given the nature of this AoS, many instruments are used in specific ways to convey particular meaning. It is vital that you have a working knowledge of the terms which follow, as well as examples of where such devices have been used and to what effect. Consider adding to the table below and making this part of your musical glossary.

> By creating your own musical glossary, similar to the one at the back of this revision guide, you will be able to cross reference quickly where musical devices occur, allowing for more effective revision.

Instrument	Technique	Used in	Effect
Violin	Glissando (up)	Herrmann – *Psycho* 'The Murder'	Screeching, stabbing, alarm, high tessitura, dissonant D♯/E
String Section	Tremolo		
Brass Section			
Woodwind Section			
Percussion Section			

Ensure you understand why the named artist uses the instruments they have chosen and what the effect of this is on the image on screen.

Harmonic analysis

Having completed the harmonic analysis questions in AoS2 (see page 57), complete the chords on the next page.

B♭   B♭7/D   E♭sus4   E♭7 A♭ F7/A B♭sus4   F   D7/F♯ Gsus2   F7   B♭

Complex chords

Composers in this genre use many types of advanced chord to create
a suitable picture for the action on screen. Complete the table below
(in C major for ease of comparison) for some of these advanced chords,
using the musical examples you have studied.

Chord	Symbol	Notation	Example
Augmented triad C – E – G♯	C+		Herrmann – *Psycho 'Prelude'*
Added 6th chord	C6		
Diminished triad			
Diminished 7th			
Half diminished 7th			

Structural considerations

Diegetic music is music which can be heard by the characters on screen – i.e. it comes from a source within the character's world. Music from instruments which are in the film (i.e. a string quartet seen playing on stage) is called **source music.**

Non-Diegetic music is music which is not present in the action on screen – i.e. the characters on screen cannot hear it. This might be **underscore** if played quietly under a scene to help establish a mood or emotional state.

Mickey-mousing is an important structural consideration which ensures that the action on screen and the music are synchronised, with specific cues or hit-points giving moments of action. This is sometimes called **parallel scoring**.

Melodic devices

The most common melodic device used in this AoS is that of the **leitmotif** – the name given to a fragment of music that represents a specific character, event or emotion. These motifs enable the music to achieve a sense of unity and development, rather than new material being constantly required.

LEITMOTIF

One of the most famous (and most thrilling) uses of leitmotif in film music is the simple semitone figure by John Williams representing the shark 'Jaws'. Starting slow, quiet and distant in the low strings, Williams portrays the approaching shark by shortening the rests between the motif, adding a gradual crescendo and developing the tessitura by including higher instruments, until finally we see the shark. The music here is entirely responsible for building suspense.

STUDY PIECE

Giacchino, *Ratatouille* 'The Paper Chase'

You can find this piece here: (from film) http://bit.ly/RatatouilleChaseScene, (from soundtrack) http://bit.ly/RatatouilleSoundtrack, (for behind-the-music video) http://bit.ly/ComposingRatatouille

Consider this chase scene from the film *Ratatouille* (2007). Here Giacchino combines large-scale orchestral writing with elements to link the music to the film – note the use of accordion to match the French setting. There are three principal themes in the film, with this piece using a developed version of the main theme: this represents Remy's hopes for the future.

The links to both the film and soundtrack are given above. How does the music enhance the action on screen? What musical devices are used? Consider using a table like the one below to write some notes before creating a more detailed response. Be sure to give examples linking to the action on screen (e.g. speech, timing, bar number if using a score) in your full response.

Action	Music	Effect
Remy runs away from Skinner	Orchestral flourish, *ff*, scurrying strings with accented lower brass. Use of crescendo, xylophone and trills in different pitches	Fast-paced, exciting, anticipation
Skinner sees Remy and accelerates on the moped	Scurrying figure made into continuous semiquavers matched with accordion chords	Use of accordion when the roads of Paris are seen
Skinner almost catches Remy but drives down stairs instead		

Listening (Section A)

Track 1 – Herrmann, *Vertigo* 'Main Theme'

Listen to this track, which you can find here: http://bit.ly/VertigoTheme

Extract: 0:00–1:05

1. What is the time signature of the extract? [1 mark]

2. A longer idea is introduced in bar 3 and repeated in bar 6.
   What interval does it use? Select one answer.

   Minor 2nd   Major 2nd   Minor 3rd   Major 3rd   [1 mark]

3. What musical device is used throughout the extract? [1 mark]

4. Which one of the following musical devices is used in the extract?

   Sequence   Contrary motion

   Appoggiatura   Chromatic scale   [1 mark]

   [Total: 4 marks]

Track 2 – Zimmer, *Angels and Demons* '160 bpm'

Listen to this track, which you can find here: http://bit.ly/160bpm

Extract: 0:20–1:20

1. What is the time signature of this extract? [1 mark]

2. Which one of these can be heard in the extract?

   Tonic pedal   Mordent   Acciaccatura   Hemiola   [1 mark]

3. Which graphic score best represents the melodic contour of
   the vocal parts?

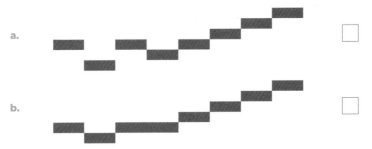

a. ☐

b. ☐

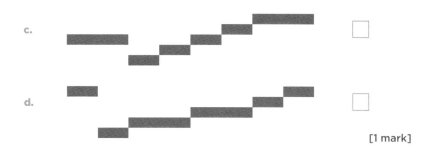

c.   ☐

d.   ☐

[1 mark]

4. The melody contains a move from an F to a G♯.
   What is the name of this interval?   [1 mark]

[Total: 4 marks]

Track 3 – Zimmer, *Pearl Harbor* 'War'

Listen to this track, which you can find here: http://bit.ly/PearlHarbourWar

Extract: 1:33–3:30

The extract is taken from a film scene where war is declared between
Japan and the USA following the attack on Pearl Harbor.

Explain how the use of musical elements enhances the audience's
understanding of the scene.   [10 marks]

This is an extended response question requiring clarity of structure.
Go through the elements in turn to create a coherent answer.

[Total for AoS3 Section A: 18 marks]

Essay question (Section C)

In the examination, you have to answer **one** essay question. There will be only one set for each AoS, so there is no choice beyond which AoS you have studied. You have 45 minutes to write the essay which is marked out of 30.

See pages 63 and 87 for more information on essay writing and assessment.

Below are two essays using the same title and similar musical examples. Use these as a comparison to help your own essay writing style.

Task – Essay Analysis

1. Read the essay by Candidate A below, marking it to the AQA mark scheme.

2. Where has the candidate gained marks? Where have marks been lost?

3. What can you learn from this candidate to prepare you for your exam?

4. Repeat points 1–3 for Candidate B's essay.

Candidate A

Compare and contrast how two contrasting named artists have created music which gives a sense of building suspense.

'Gladiator' is an epic story about a gladiator who is wronged and tries to get vengeance from the Roman emperor who has wronged him and killed his family. Maximus is denied his place as leader of the empire by the ambitious son of the dead emperor who kills his family. He is then captured by slavers and forced to fight as a gladiator by the slave masters. Because he was in the military and is a good fighter Maximus wins each local competition, eventually going to Rome to compete in the Colosseum where he battles lots of well-known fighters. The emperor, jealous of Maximus' fighting, challenges him to a duel to put the threat to his throne down, but decides to stab him in the torso to throw the fight in his favour. However, Maximus ultimately wins the fight and kills the emperor.

The first piece of music I would like to talk about comes from the opening battle scene. The music is in D minor and sometimes changes to the relative major G major. The melody goes A-D-E-F which has a minor 6th interval and sounds sad. However, the strings make the music sound majestic which suits the Roman army. About a minute in, we realise that Maximus' peace deal to the Barbarians has been rejected and preparation for battle starts. A male voice sings a creepy melodic line using semitones and then the music gets faster and louder making it more excited. Herrmann then copies Holst's Mars by writing in 5/4 and using motor rhythms and was later sued for plagiarism. Trumpets and drums are used to make it sound like a battle. Trills and crescendos add interest. As the battle starts the main theme comes back to remind us it is the main theme and cross-rhythms make the piece sound angry and scary. As the battle is won by the Roman soldiers the music moves to C major using pedal points. It does not sound too happy though as, even though the Romans won the battle, many of them died. There is a modal ending Em – Am.

Zimmer also creates suspense in Inception 'Dream is Collapsing'. The music starts on an electric guitar and gradually adds strings in. The melody repeats a single note lots of times and on the first beat of every other 3/4 bar uses the semitone below in a slurred fashion. The harmony is often minor and unrelated. The texture gradually gets thicker by adding more instruments – strings using cross-rhythms, then horns, then percussion – until the music climaxes and changes key with a huge slow down. As the music stops the atmosphere, which has been made dark and oppressive, clears.

Candidate B

Compare and contrast how two contrasting named artists have created music which gives a sense of building suspense.

Hans Zimmer's music to Gladiator greatly enhances the visual plot, using leitmotif, ethnic instruments and driving rhythms to support the on-screen action. The opening 'battle scene' is an action scene with minimal dialogue, allowing the non-diegetic music to come to the fore in supporting and enhancing the plot. Similarly, Bernard Herrmann creates horrific suspense in his music for the film Psycho, with 'The Cellar' being one of the most terrifying moments of the film.

The Gladiator battle scene opens with the main theme, a four-bar long majestic rising D minor idea spanning a minor 6th (A-D-E-F) performed on the horns with gentle percussive ostinato accompaniment. This theme is of utmost importance to the film, acting as a leitmotif throughout and, importantly, appearing at the very end of the film. A modulation to the relative major, F major, and use of dominant pedal (on C) allows for a subtle development of the idea. Greater use of chords, complete with 4-3 and 9-8 suspensions and a rising chromatic violin line, allows for the music to move towards a change in the scene; as Maximus, the central protagonist of the film, answers the Barbarian call for war he declares 'unleash hell'. The music suitably follows suit with an immediate change in temperature. A male voice replaces the alto female vocals heard at the very start of the film, using increased chromaticism in his nonsense syllables (F-E-F-G#), with the dissonance of the G# helping to move away from the diatonic landscape. The regular ostinato figures presented up to this point are avoided, matching the unpredictable tension of the plot.

As the build to battle commences, the music gains energy from an increase in tempo with the chromatic male vocal line now presented as an ostinato in the lower strings complete with brass hunting calls and bass pedal points. Cross-rhythms, accented weak beats and even a temporary move to 5/4 time (evoking Holst's Mars) all give a sense of excitement and action to the plot, creating a victorious second theme. String trills, surging crescendo and dramatic twists with fragments of melodic material create anxiety – the Barbarians are putting up a good fight despite the Roman army being better prepared.

A tonal shift to C major and to 3/4 time, complete with the opening leitmotif, marks a turning point in the battle, even though the action on screen continues unabated despite the slow motion effect.

The expansive use of strings using dotted minims, with dominant pedal points which resolve to the submediant rather than the tonic, gives a feeling of space and suspensions, including the Lydian #4-3, evoking feelings of loss. The driving second theme, central to the battle, remains absent, and the scene ends on a bare 5th A chord, suggesting the battle is far from over despite the apparent Roman victory.

Herrmann masters the dramatic role of tension and release in his music to the film Psycho. As the film reaches its famous conclusion with the identity of Mrs Bates being revealed, the music represents the confusion and horror of the characters. As Lila moves towards the cellar, the music is filled with scurrying and quite random chromatic quaver figures in the cellos, containing disjunct leaps. The addition of violas and violins gradually raises the tessitura, though this is a gradual process with the focus being on rapid heavy bowing of the instruments to create a sense of unease. The double basses often play a semitone motif with accents and staccato, with this idea also being treated to rhythmic augmentation (quavers to crotchets and then dotted minims). However, rather than continuously raise the tension and level of suspense, Herrmann actually dissipates the musical energy, writing a descending chromatic scale as Lila descends the stairs which awkwardly resolves on to an A major 7 chord which is passed up the strings – ending on a top C# in the violins, complete with tremolo. This is just at the point that Lila's hand reaches for Mrs Bates.

As Mrs Bates' chair turns, revealing her to be a mummified corpse, Lila screams which directly leads into a repeat of 'The Murder' scene, which now acts as a leitmotif for the stabbing attack. The violins each have their own part playing highly dissonant chords, complete with a slight upward glissando. The high tessitura and dissonance achieved by the separation of parts is iconic of a scream, with the physical action of the playing style representing a stabbing motion. The music to both of these contrasting scenes is central to the communication of the plot to the audience; not only does the music link to the action on screen, it actively enhances it, evoking previous memories and looking forward in the unfolding plot, creating and releasing tension and suspense.

AoS3 KEY TERMS: A SUMMARY

Melody: leitmotif

Harmony/Tonality: power chords, sus4 chords, chord extensions/ symbols, complex chords, tonic and dominant pedal, tonal, atonal, modal

Structure: cue, underscore, soundtrack, mickey-mousing, source music, diegetic and non-diegetic music

Sonority/Timbre: standard orchestral and jazz, rock and pop instruments, electronic instruments, ethnic instruments, technological effects, tremolo

Texture: cluster, polarized texture, drone

Tempo, metre and rhythm: metronome mark, additive rhythm, cross rhythm, rhythmic layering

Music for theatre

Introduction

Broadway, the West End, and all the many theatres in between – this AoS looks at how music can be used to entertain audiences across the globe.

There are five named composers in this AoS for you to listen to, study and gain a critical appreciation of. Notice that the specification cites that this is defined as 'music composed to govern, enhance or support a theatrical conception from 1930 to the present'. While *The Threepenny Opera* can be seen as being originally composed earlier than this, the first film was completed after this and so it can be used for the specification.

- Kurt Weill
- Richard Rodgers
- Stephen Sondheim
- Claude-Michel Schönberg
- Jason Robert Brown

Some of the key vocabulary for this AoS is shared with others; it is advisable to work through those exercises in the previous chapters *before* starting on the work in this chapter to help develop your musical skills fully.

The AQA A Level Music specification can be found at www.aqa.org. uk/subjects/music/as-and-a-level/music-7272. This contains a full list of the relevant vocabulary for each AoS. Further examples and explanations can be found in the *AQA AS and A Level Music Study Guide* (Rhinegold Education).

Score reading exercise

STUDY PIECE 1

Schönberg, *Les Miserables* 'Bring Him Home'
You can find this piece here: http://bit.ly/LesMisBHH

This exercise requires access to a score of the piece which cannot be reproduced here for copyright reasons. It can be purchased online from Musicnotes, where the main features of the song are notated clearly. There are many recordings of this piece; it is usually performed in A major, but various transpositions exist to allow other voice types to be able to perform it.

A section (Instrumental and 'God on High')
Consider the first part of the song and mark up your score. You may wish to differentiate between musical elements when writing your ideas down to aid revision.

Melody:

- If the sung melody is syllabic or melismatic
- Any portamento use (vocal glissando) – whether notated or completed in performance
- Any intervals of importance (e.g. because of their repetition)
- Is the melody conjunct or disjunct? Are there any specific (angular) jumps?

Rhythm:

- Any rhythms of importance and why these might occur

Harmony:

- Any chord extensions (6th, 7th, 9th, 11th, 13th and so on) and how these are voiced
- Any chromatic harmony (such as diminished 7th chords, augmented chords) or chromatic countermelodies
- Any passing modulations (look out for the new leading note as an accidental)

Tempo:

- What tempo the piece is – spotting if it changes and what the metronome mark is

Texture:

- The role of the chorus and instrumental backing

B section ('He's like the son I might have known')

Contrast is given in this new section with a change in melodic character. Continue marking up your score, using the note-taking system you used for the introduction.

- How is the melodic line different to the A section? Is there any use of motif? Are these developed? How?
- Analyse the chord sequence; which chords are not closely related to the tonic key?
- What is the role of the following instruments in this section? Highlight your findings on your score.
  - Cello
  - Harp
  - Violins
  - Bass

A section ('Bring Him Peace')

This repetition of earlier material is developed to enhance the character. Consider the following:

- Are there any new melodic ideas? What is the effect of these?
- Are any suspensions used? If so, where are they used and why are they used at that point?
- Has the use of instruments changed?
- How is the section developed?
- Which section has a greater emotional impact? What features of the music enable this?

Coda ('Let me Die, Let him Live')

This acts as the final section of the song based upon the original A section material. Compare this section with the music that has come before, thinking about:

- Melody: the tessitura, use of rhythms, phrase structure, use of fermata
- Harmony: how are extended chords used? Are there any pedal points?
- Texture: how do the final four bars change texturally? Link this to the plot
- Effect: what is the effect of this passage on the audience?

Summary

Approaching musical analysis in this way is a great way to get to know lots of musical detail about a piece of music, enabling you to write with musical conviction in the examination and improve your musical ear. More importantly, it allows for close musical analysis which allows you to write with musical confidence rather than simply describing the plot.

Aural analysis exercise

This alternative approach can be taken where a score is not available, using your ear to refine how the composer uses the musical elements in a piece of music by listening to the piece four times in total, focussing on different elements as you listen.

1st playing	■ **Sonority (Timbre):** number, type, family, relationship, special techniques? ■ **Tonality:** major, minor, modal, atonal? ■ **Rhythm:** time signature, tempo (bpm), metronome mark (mm) ■ **Structure:** do any sections repeat? Are they developed?
2nd playing	■ **Melody:** conjunct, disjunct, leitmotif, syllabic, melismatic, pitch bend ■ **Rhythm:** ostinato, riff ■ **Harmony:** chromatic chords, suspensions, chord extensions, cadences ■ **Tonality:** are there any modulations? Link to structure
3rd playing	■ **Harmony:** harmonic rhythm ■ **Melody:** articulation, phrase structure ■ **Texture:** changes, link to word painting, a cappella, colla voce ■ **Style:** period, plot, purpose
4th playing	■ **Confirm all points** above and add detail, making references to the structure and/or text

STUDY PIECE 2

Weill, *Rise and Fall of the City of Mahagonny* 'Alabama Song'

You can find this song here: http://bit.ly/AlabamaSongKW

Using the steps from the listening table above, listen to the music in the link and aurally analyse the piece of music in the boxes below.

Try to complete this work on your own, giving a few minutes between each performance. At the end, compare your work with that of your peers to facilitate a discussion. Add in any extra points they might have, then compare to the suggestions in the Answers section at the back of the book. How does your response compare?

1st playing	
2nd playing	
3rd playing	
4th playing	

Comparison

This song was also recorded by David Bowie and The Doors. Listen to both performances and compare them to the original 1930 recording.

The Doors, 'Alabama Song': http://bit.ly/AlabamaSongTD

David Bowie, 'Alabama Song': http://bit.ly/AlabamaSongDB

1st playing	
2nd playing	
3rd playing	
4th playing	

Listening (Section A)

Track 1 – Rodgers, *Sound of Music* 'Edelweiss'

Listen to this song, which you can find here: http://bit.ly/EdelweissSOM

Extract: 0:00–0:39

1. The introduction contains four bars. Complete the chord for the fourth bar in the box below using Roman numerals. [2 marks]

Bar 1	Bar 2	Bar 3	Bar 4
Ic	Ic	IVsus2	

2. What is the tonality of the extract?

   Major   **Minor**   **Atonal**   **Modal** [1 mark]

3. Underline **one** statement which is true about the first 16 bars of the vocal line in this extract.

   a. The vocal line is melismatic with no blue notes

   b. The vocal line is melismatic with blue notes

   c. The vocal line is syllabic with no blue notes

   d. The vocal line is syllabic with blue notes [1 mark]

[Total: 4 marks]

Track 2 – Sondheim, *Into the Woods* 'Agony'

Listen to this song, which you can find here: http://bit.ly/AgonyITW

Extract: 0:00-0:50

1   Did I abuse **her or** show her disdain?

2   Why does she run **from me**?

3   If I should lose **her how** shall I regain

4   The heart she has won **from me**?

1.   What is the time signature of this song?   [1 mark]

2.   The cello plays prominently the opening melody. Which interval
     does it play in the opening three bars? Underline your answer.

    Minor 2nd   **Major 2nd**   **Minor 3rd**   **Major 3rd**   [1 mark]

3.   The vocal line is often divided into one-bar phrases.
     What is the interval sung on the words highlighted in bold above?
     Underline your answer.

    Perfect 4th   **Perfect 5th**   **Minor 6th**   **Major 6th**   [1 mark]

4.   Later in the piece a flute solo can be heard (from 0:38).
     This solo includes a note which does **not** belong to the tonic key.
     How can you analyse this note?   [1 mark]

[Total: 4 marks]

Track 3 – Jason Robert Brown, *Songs for a New World* 'Christmas Lullaby'

Listen to this song, which you can find here: http://bit.ly/ChristmasLullaby

Extract: 0:00-1:55

The extract is taken from a scene where a woman has just discovered
she is pregnant. She sings this song where she compares herself to
the Virgin Mary.

Explain how the use of musical elements enhances the audience's
understanding of the scene.   [10 marks]

[Total for AoS4 Section A: 18 marks]

Essay question (Section C)

In the examination, you have to answer one essay question. There will be only one set for each AoS so there is no choice beyond which AoS you have studied. You have **45 minutes** to write the essay which is marked out of **30**.

See page 63 for more information on essay writing and assessment.

Consider the essay question on the next page, planning your response before embarking on the writing process. Think about which musical examples will best allow you to respond to the question:

- **Introduction** – address the question, introduce the two pieces used to answer the question

- **Main Essay** – are you going to talk extensively about the first piece in one paragraph and the second in another? Or are you going to compare directly both pieces side by side, element by element? How might the wording of the question help you to decide?

- **Conclusion** – have you answered the question?

Having established your basic plan, give thought to your essay style. A good set of rules to follow are:

1. **Keep the introduction short**, reusing language from the question to help focus your argument on answering the question. Avoid excessive non-musical context which wastes precious time and struggles to be awarded marks.

2. Start each paragraph with a **short analytical point** which answers the question.

3. Back up this point with **evidence** from the music you have chosen.

4. Avoid simply describing the music, but instead give **analytical detail**, evaluating the effect of a particular musical device rather than simply stating its presence.

5. Start a new paragraph for a new point, following points 2–4.

6. Keep your conclusion short, addressing the question. Avoid simply repeating the points you have already made – try and save something new to say to give your essay a real sense of style.

Using music by two different composers, consider how they have written music with contrasting emotional states. You should refer to at least one piece of music by each different named composer.

Introduction 1

'Empty Chairs at Empty Tables' from Les Miserables (Schonberg) and 'Oklahoma!' from Oklahoma (Rodgers) are two contrasting songs from different musicals. Both pieces come at the end of the second act but have different emotions.

Introduction 2

The two songs I have chosen to write about in this essay are 'Empty Chairs' from Les Miserables by Schonberg and 'Oklahoma!' from Oklahoma (Rodgers). Both are contrasting: 'Empty Chairs' is a solo sung by Marius who is distraught following the death of many of his friends, whereas 'Oklahoma!' is an upbeat chorus number filled with excitement and hope for the future.

Introduction task

Read both introductions opposite; both contain relevant information, but could have a greater sense of essay style. Rewrite the introduction using this information and the guidance from page 87. How does your introduction compare to that of your peers?

Writing the essay

The points in the table below are the musical features that could be used to write your essay. Using these points and your own analysis, write the essay, trying to follow style steps 1–6 from page 87. Consider if there are any other pieces by these named composers which would help your work.

'Empty Chairs at Empty Tables'	'Oklahoma!'
▪ Melancholy, lonely, regret ▪ Solo Tenor, sotto voce ▪ 32-bar song form (adapted) ▪ A sections ('there's a grief') harmonically unadventurous (harmonic rhythm = 1 chord per bar) ▪ B section ('at the table') faster harmonic rhythm (two chords per bar) and move to relative major C major ▪ Use of perfect cadences, extensions, 7ths, broken chords (9ths) ▪ Modulates to C♯m (tertiary relationship to Am) – impact ▪ Conjunct melody, falling through 5th, some disjunct moments ▪ Melody and accompaniment – word painting 'lonely barricade' as bass drops out ▪ Constant quavers at close – movement and momentum	▪ Excitement, anticipation ▪ Solo tenor with chorus ▪ ABACDE structure (from second special chorus) ▪ Rich 7-part vocal texture ▪ Ascending scales – excitement ▪ Diminished 7th ('honey lamb') ▪ Hoedown feel ('yippy yi') over dominant pedal ▪ Bass ostinato D C B A ▪ Gradual outline of D major 7 to 'Oklahoma' – move to G major ▪ Use of perfect cadences, circle of 5ths ▪ Use of pause at close ▪ Use of full chorus – all on stage; starts with solos before full chorus join in ▪ Dynamic contrasts including use of crescendo

AoS4 KEY TERMS: A SUMMARY

Melody: pitch bend, melisma, syllabic, slide, glissando, leitmotif, angular

Harmony: power chords, sus4 chords, chord extensions, complex chords, chord symbols

Structure: intro/outro, bridge, verse, chorus, instrumental, middle 8

Sonority/Timbre: studio/technological effects, orchestral and contemporary instruments, vocal timbres, specific instrumental techniques

Texture: a cappella, colla voce

Tempo, metre and rhythm: bpm, metronome mark, irregular metre

Jazz

Introduction

From 'cool' to 'hot', the music of this Area of Study is richly rewarding.

There are six named artists in this AoS for you to listen to, study and gain a critical appreciation of. Notice that the specification cites that Jazz is defined as 'a style of music characterised by a strong but flexible rhythmic understructure with solo and ensemble improvisations on basic tunes and chord patterns and a highly sophisticated harmonic idiom from 1920 to the present'.

- Louis Armstrong
- Duke Ellington
- Charlie Parker
- Miles Davis
- Pat Metheny
- Gwilym Simcock

Some of the key vocabulary for this AoS is shared with others; it is advisable to work through the exercises in the previous chapters *before* starting on the work in this chapter to help develop your musical skills fully.

The AQA A Level Music specification can be found at www.aqa.org. uk/subjects/music/as-and-a-level/music-7272. This contains a full list of the relevant vocabulary for each AoS. Further examples and explanations can be found in the *AQA AS and A Level Music Study Guide* (Rhinegold Education).

Jazz and Blues featured as an optional unit in the old AQA A Level (Unit 4); you may therefore find there are still resources online for that legacy specification which may be useful to develop your understanding.

AoS5 MUSICAL LANGUAGE

Musical language for this Area of Study

Melodic features

Jazz is made by the improvisatory nature of the music, with a whole host of melodic devices being used. For the extracts below, consider which of the following melodic devices you can hear, writing in the box next to the extract:

- **Glissando**
- **Pitch-bend**
- **Smear**
- **Spill/fall-off**
- **Rip**
- **Mordent**
- **Triplet**
- **Ghost note**
- **Acciaccatura**

Extract 1	Duke Ellington, 'Don't Mean a Thing' http://bit.ly/ DukeEllington1943
Extract 2	Charlie Parker, 'All the Things You Are' http://bit.ly/ CharlieParkerATTYA
Extract 3	Louis Armstrong, 'Dream a Little Dream' http://bit.ly/ LouisArmstrongDALD

Blues scales

There are three principal types of **blues scale** – the **hexatonic** (6-note), **heptatonic** (7-note) and **nonatonic** (9-note). The description of each is given below.

Using this description, write in the correct accidentals on the score to match the description.

Hexatonic: 6-note scale

- Formed of a minor **pentatonic** scale
- Added ♯4th (sometimes notated as ♭5th)

Heptatonic: 7-note scale

- **Diatonic** scale
- Evokes the minor mode – minor 3rd, 5th and 7th

Nonatonic: 9-note scale

- **Diatonic** major scale with 2 additional notes
- Added minor 3rd
- Added minor 7th

Extended chords

Extended chords are made by adding notes to the basic major or minor triad.

Tonic (I) – Mediant (III) – Dominant (V) = Triad

The word 'mediant' comes from the Latin 'to be in the middle' – the third is in the middle of the tonic and dominant to make the triad.

These added notes often go up in thirds from the dominant:

Tonic – Mediant – Dominant – 7th – 9th – 11th – 13th

If we use the scale of the chord we wish to extend, this gives us the notes we can use to extend the chord. These scales can include major or minor, or more complex patterns such as the seven musical **modes** or a **diminished** (**octatonic**) scale. The table below shows how these chords are constructed using this process, using the **mixolydian** mode.

Chord Voicing

Working out the correct notes for the extended chord is the first part of the process. However, if you play the chords above they will probably not sound as exotic as similar chords used in jazz standards. This is to do with how the chord has been voiced – that is to say, how the chord is ordered, spaced and constructed.

A good example of this point is the opening bars of Miles Davis's 'Four':

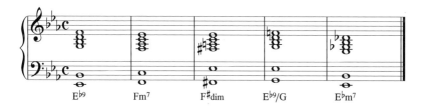

Eb9   Fm7   F#dim   Eb9/G   Ebm7

Notice how there is a sense of contrary motion between the top and bass of the chord, using inversions, extended chords and a diminished chord.

Experiment with voicing these extended chords in different ways. Why might Davis have voiced these chords in this way? If the tempo and style was more 'cool' jazz, how might the voicings have changed?

STUDY PIECE 1

Miles Davis, 'I Fall in Love Too Easily'

You can find this song here: http://bit.ly/MilesDavisIFILTE

This is a beautiful ballad-style cover of the original 1944 song composed by Jule Styne. Davis recorded many different covers of this song and this could form a useful starting point for your own analysis.

As you listen to the track, consider:

- The interaction between piano and trumpet
- What instrumental techniques are used
- How the original melody is developed
- How the solos compare to each other

STUDY PIECE 2

Gwilym Simcock, 'Cry Me a River'
Available on Spotify: http://bit.ly/GwilymSimcock

Simcock's superb blend of classical, popular and jazz is evidenced in this cover of 'Cry Me a River', with softness of touch to the performance as a whole. As you listen, think about how the music creates and releases tension, weaving the melody in and out of increasingly elaborate improvisations. Listen out especially for the improvisations in the bass which add real depth to the piece.

STUDY PIECE 3

Pat Metheny, 'Are you going with me?'
You can find this song here: http://bit.ly/PatMethenyAYGWM

This piece clearly demonstrates the Latin influences on 1980s American jazz, with some exciting solos performed on a synthesiser over a repeating bass riff. Listen out for the following:

0:00   bass riff, use of synthesiser, chilled vibe established, increasing in musical temperature

2:08   solo synthesiser over bass riff; note the use of modulation and pitch bend

3:35   solo synth adds in second melodic part before a drum fill

3:44   upwards move to a new key centre for guitar solo (Roland)

5:00   addition of light backing vocals on nonsense syllables

5:20   another modulation upwards building excitement as the guitar explores its upper register

6:25   musical climax, combining synth, guitar and backing vocals

8:00   guitar cadenza

8:40   piano scalic flourish with fade out

You may wish to complete a more extensive aural analysis of all three of these pieces; if so, consider using the approach outlined on page 83.

Listening (Section A)

Track 1 – Louis Armstrong, 'Nobody Knows'

Listen to this track, which you can find here: http://bit.ly/LouisArmstrongNKTTIS

Extract: 2:06–2:36

1. What is the interval between the notes sung to 'No-bo' from 'Nobody knows' at the start of the extract? [1 mark]

2. Which **two** of these devices are used in the extract? Underline your answers.

   Syllabic   **Melisma**   **Spread chord**

   Sequence   **Pizzicato**   [2 marks]

3. What cadence does the piece end on?   [1 mark]

[Total: 4 marks]

Track 2 – Charlie Parker, 'Summertime'

Listen to this track, which you can find here: http://bit.ly/CharlieParkerSummertime

Extract: 0:00–0:40

1. What is the range of notes covered when the saxophone first plays? [1 mark]

2. What harmonic device can be heard in the extract? Underline your answer.

   Blues notes   **Pedal point**   **Sequence**   **Ostinato**   [1 mark]

3. Towards the end of the extract, what changes in the rhythm of the stringed instruments? [1 mark]

4. At the end of the extract, how are the upper strings played?

   Pizzicato   **Tremolo**   **Arco**   **Col legno**   [1 mark]

[Total: 4 marks]

Track 3 – Miles Davis, 'All Blues'

Listen to this track, which you can find here: http://bit.ly/AllBluesMilesDavis

Extract: 0:00–2:12

What elements of Cool Jazz can be heard in this extract? [10 marks]

Essay question (Section C)

In the examination, you have to answer one essay question. There will be only one set for each AoS, so there is no choice beyond which AoS you have studied. You have 45 minutes to write the essay which is marked out of 30.

See pages 63 and 87 for more information on essay writing and assessment.

Consider the essay title below, planning your response to it. The first section of the essay, looking at two pieces by Miles Davis, 'Four' and 'All Blues', has been started.

Choosing two of the named artists, comment on how their music has achieved stylistic variety. You should discuss instrumentation, harmony and melody, as appropriate.

Miles Davis 'Four'

Written for a jazz quintet (trumpet, tenor sax, piano, bass and drum kit) the 1964 recording of 'Four' exemplifies Davis' reworking of his earlier Bebop style, using a fast tempo and some exceptionally complex instrumental writing. These include a fast walking bass on the double bass, played pizzicato, and very fast comping on the piano using a variety of extended chords. The drum kit also has some virtuosic moments with fast ride cymbal rhythms and occasional rim shots. The harmonic vocabulary is complex, as expected for the genre of Jazz. Whilst the basic harmonic progression could be analysed in a simplistic fashion (the opening four bars, for example, could be seen as being in the tonic Eb major), it is Davis' use of substitution chords and extensions which make the harmonic language complex. This includes the chromatic Eb9 – Fm7 – F#°– Eb9/G (first inversion) – Ebm7 of the opening which effectively moves to the tonic minor at the end of the 4-bar phrase as well as a similar chromatic movement from Gm7 – F#m7 – Fm7 – Bb7 which follows. This gives a standard ii–V turnaround to allow the main idea to start again. Davis uses sequences and improvisation in the melody, with the choruses having a wider range.

Miles Davis 'All Blues'

Whereas 'Four' evokes more of a hot jazz style, 'All Blues' epitomises cool jazz, using modal harmonies and restrained improvisations. Written for solo trumpet, alto and tenor saxophone, bass, drums and piano, the jazz idiom is again redefined to create stylistic variety. The piece uses G mixolydian extensively, making alterations to the standard changes by substituting chord V with an Eb7#9 chord, giving a flattened 6th turnaround. Riffs are used extensively, including a piano trill which blurs the texture, a saxophone riff in 3rds used as a linking section and a bass riff which is performed throughout the piece except where chord V or bvi harmony is explored (bars 9 and 10 of the chorus).

Task 1: Second Named Artist

Complete a similar comparison for another named artist looking at two contrasting pieces. Be sure to analyse your points and use comparative language.

Task 2: Editing the First Named Artist

Rewrite the two paragraphs on Miles Davis, creating two paragraphs in your own words. You may wish to use the two pieces selected in the example above, or use different pieces.

Task 3: Essay Technique

Write an introduction and conclusion to finish the piece of work. See the AoS2, AoS3 and AoS4 chapters for further guidance on essay writing.

Task 4: Assessment

Mark your essay to the mark scheme and compare it with essays written by your peers. If they have achieved better marks than you, work out why this is and try to incorporate these ideas into your own work.

AoS5 KEY TERMS: A SUMMARY

Melody: glissando, pitch-bend, smear, spill/fall-off, rip

Harmony: chord extensions, added note chords, substitution (including tritone substitution), jazz symbols, turn-around

Tonality: blue notes, blues scale, pentatonic scale, octatonic (diminished) scale, modes

Structure: 12-bar blues, chord changes, song form/standard form, middle 8/bridge, intro/outro, head, chorus, fours, break

Sonority/Timbre: growl/talking trumpet, harmon mute, wah-wah mute, ghosted notes, slap bass, rim-shot, standard big-band instruments

Texture: a cappella, heterophonic

Tempo, metre and rhythm: swing and straight rhythm, cross rhythms, push and drag, double time, ametrical, riff, stop time

Contemporary traditional music

Introduction

Taking something old and making it into something new is a cornerstone of artistic endeavour. This Area of Study takes an ethnomusicological approach to five different musical fusions.

There are five named artists in this AoS for you to listen to, study and gain a critical appreciation of. The specification cites that music in this genre is defined as 'music influenced by traditional musical features fused with contemporary elements and styles'.

- Astor Piazzolla

- Toumani Diabaté

- Anoushka Shankar

- Mariza

- Bellowhead

As with the previous AoS, the exercises in this chapter will help with specific revision as well as helping to develop your general musicianship.

The AQA A Level Music specification can be found at www.aqa.org. uk/subjects/music/as-and-a-level/music-7272. This contains a full list of the relevant vocabulary for each AoS. Further examples and explanations can be found in the *AQA AS and A Level Music Study Guide* (Rhinegold Education).

Contemporary v traditional

With this AoS it is vital to understand how the named artists are using traditional musical ideas in a more contemporary way. Below are examples of how you could approach this revision.

Tango and Piazzolla

Piazzolla is credited by many musicologists as being the father of *Tango Nuevo* ('new tango'), taking an older tradition and adding new ideas to it. In Piazzolla's own words, 'my tango does meet the present'.

Traditional elements ('tango')	Contemporary elements ('tango nuevo')
■ $\frac{4}{4}$ time ■ use of accents, including on weak beats ■ **syncopation** ■ **ostinato** – often 3+3+2 quavers ■ melancholy – minor key ■ strong dynamic contrasts ■ a singer often features – sad lyrics ■ bass often playing on beats 1 and 4	Based on traditional tango, but: ■ singer avoided – instrumental (sometimes including electric guitar and drum kit) ■ greater influence from jazz and later rock/pop music ■ Chromatic extensions ■ specific instrumental techniques to achieve new timbral colours

Piazzola's 'Tango Sensations' wonderfully demonstrates the reworking of the traditional form to make a contemporary idiom. In this piece, performed with string quartet, the tango gains a programmatic element to represent fear.

You can find it here: http://bit.ly/PiazzollaFear

Listen out for:

■ The **fugal** use of the main melody, initially played on the bandoneon

■ Use of **upper auxiliary** notes

■ The minor tonality with unexpected **modulations**

■ The use of **additive rhythms** – 3+3+2 permeating the texture with cross-rhythms

■ Use of **pitch bends** in the melody

■ The way the instruments are played, e.g. **stab chords** on the bandoneon, string techniques

The use of instruments in specific ways – particularly stringed instruments – is central to Piazzolla's sound world. The specification requires you to have a working knowledge of these. Revise these terms by listening to the extracts and completing the table below:

Name	Evidence	Description
Chicharra	http://bit.ly/Chicharra	
Latigo	http://bit.ly/TangoLatigo	
Arrastre	http://bit.ly/Arrastre	
Tambor	http://bit.ly/TangoTambor	
Golpe de Caja	http://bit.ly/GalopeDeCaja	

An excellent guide to string techniques can be found at http://bit.ly/StringTechniquesLSO where some members of the LSO guide you through various different playing techniques. This would also be invaluable for composition work.

Fado and Mariza

The fado tradition has many similarities with tango, and artists have also been quick to take the tradition and add a contemporary twist. Mariza has brought the tradition to a more global audience by combining the traditions of fado with Iberian pop music.

The following two pieces show the traditional and the contemporary for fado. As you listen to them, consider how they are similar and different, completing a table to show your working. A few starting points are given here:

STUDY PIECE 1

Traditional – Argentina Santos, 'Maria Severa'

Listen to this track, which you can find here: http://bit.ly/MariaSevera

Listen for the traditional ensemble using Portuguese guitars; the fluctuations between major and minor chords; and drama added with tempo changes at the end of each verse.

STUDY PIECE 2

Contemporary – Mariza, 'Alma'

Listen to this track, which you can find here: http://bit.ly/MarizaAlma

Consider the influence of Iberian pop music – the modern production techniques; the use of pop conventions; the regularity of tempo, $\frac{4}{4}$ time and harmonic rhythm.

English folk music and Bellowhead

Famous for reviving the English folk tradition, Bellowhead take traditional folk pieces including sea shanties, jigs and songs and put a contemporary focus on them.

In a similar way to the Mariza exercise above, listen to one of Bellowhead's songs, comparing the traditional with the contemporary. The example opposite, using the sea shanty tradition, can be used to help you with your independent analysis. Fill in the rest of the boxes with your own analysis.

Traditional – Roll the Woodpile Down http://bit.ly/RollTheWoodpileDown	Bellowhead – Roll the Woodpile Down http://bit.ly/BellowheadRTWD
■ Solo/chorus in call and response ■ $\frac{4}{4}$ with moderate tempo	■ Greater use of independent melodic lines ■ Solo/chorus in call and response

Indian raga and Anoushka Shankar

Anoushka Shankar is famous for being classically trained in the art of Indian raga performance, playing the sitar, as well as establishing herself as a contemporary solo musician. Shankar comes from a very musical family: her father, the late Ravi Shankar, is renowned across the globe for his raga performances, and her half-sister is the singer-songwriter Norah Jones. Anoushka Shankar's music often shows great levels of collaboration, having recorded traditional Indian music as well as more contemporary pieces as a solo artist.

Below are links to two recordings by Shankar – one where she is performing a traditional Hindustani piece, and another where she has fused her training with a more contemporary sound world to compose her own music. Listen to both tracks and consider how the traditional is fused with the contemporary, completing the table on the next page. The answers section at the back of the book has some suggestions to focus your ideas.

Traditional – 'Rag Desh'

http://bit.ly/RagDesh

Contemporary – 'Land of Gold' (with Alev Lenz)

http://bit.ly/LandOfGoldAS

Traditional raga elements	Contemporary elements
▪ Use of raga ▪ Use of tihais (3 repetitions)	▪ Fusion of instruments – cello, vocals in English, hang drum

Kora music and Toumani Diabaté

Hailing from a very long line of kora players, Diabaté combines traditional kora performance with more contemporary genres like jazz, blues and flamenco. In a similar way to Shankar, he freely crosses the boundary between traditional and contemporary music. Three examples of this fusion of musical styles are given below. Consider analysing the music following the steps given above to gain an appreciation of the music.

'Songhai 2' (Diabaté with Spanish flamenco group Ketama)

http://bit.ly/KetamaTD

'Bamako' from *Malicool* (Diabaté with American jazz trombonist Roswell Rudd)

http://bit.ly/BamakoTD

'Queen Bee' from *Kulanjan* (Diabaté with blues artist Taj Mahal)

http://bit.ly/QueenBeeTD

Listening (Section A)

Track 1 – Anoushka Shankar, 'Prayer in Passing'

Listen to this song, which you can find here: http://bit.ly/PrayerInPassingAS

Extract: 0:00–1:20

1. What is the name given to the constant note at the bottom of
   the texture?   [1 mark]

2. Which term below best describes the piano playing style?

   Rubato   **Tremolo**   **Vibrato**   **Glissando**   [1 mark]

3. The veena plays a solo from 0:29, starting on a D. What interval
   does it play prominently?

   Minor 2nd   **Major 2nd**   **Perfect 4th**   **Perfect 5th**   [1 mark]

4. This track includes non-musical sounds. What is this
   process called?   [1 mark]

                                                            [Total: 4 marks]

Track 2 – Mariza, 'Retrato'

Listen to this song, which you can find here: http://bit.ly/MarizaRetrato

Extract: 2:25–3:35

1. Suggest a suitable time signature for this extract.

   $\frac{3}{4}$ $\frac{4}{4}$ $\frac{6}{8}$ $\frac{9}{8}$ [1 mark]

2. Which term best describes the chords heard at 2:34?

   Diminished   **Augmented**   **Tierce de Picardie**   **Minor**   [1 mark]

3. Aside from the piano, which other instrument can be heard in
   the extract?   [1 mark]

4. On what extended chord does the extract end?   [1 mark]

                                                            [Total: 4 marks]

Track 3 – Piazzolla, 'Anxiety'

Listen to this piece, which you can find here: http://bit.ly/PiazzollaAnxiety

Extract: 0:00–2:08

The excerpt is called 'Anxiety'. How are the elements of music
used to evoke this title?   [10 marks]

Essay question (Section C)

In the examination, you have to answer one essay
question. There will be only one set for each AoS
so there is no choice beyond which AoS you have
studied. You have 45 minutes to write the essay which
is marked out of 30.

See pages 63 and 87 for more information on essay writing
and assessment.

For two named artists you have studied, discuss how they have developed
a traditional style for a contemporary audience.

This is a fairly standard question for this AoS, and certainly one you need to
practise and be able to address fully. It is also an excellent question to approach
for revision for each of the named artists.

Sample assessment papers showing how the exam will be laid out and
practice questions can be found on the AQA website at www.aqa.org.
uk/subjects/music/as-and-a-level/music-7272/assessment-resources

As you approach this essay, remember the guidance given in the
previous chapters which have discussed approaches to writing the
essay as well as looking at how to style your work.

Indicative content: Astor Piazzolla

Born in Argentina, 1921. Fused Argentine Tango with Jazz and Classical music to create 'tango nuevo' – new tango.

'Milonga del Ángel' http://bit.ly/MilongaDelAngelAP	'Yo soy Maria' http://bit.ly/YoSoyMaria
▪ Milonga – from the slow tempo tradition ▪ **Ternary form** ABA + Intro ▪ **Habanera rhythm** outlining tonic/dominant in bass ▪ Use of C♯ in violin – **pitch bending**, use of sul G ▪ Bandoneon solo (crescendo) ▪ Repeat changes – violin high octave ▪ Improvised feel ▪ **Syncopation** ▪ Instrument techniques – bellow vibrato on bandoneon, **glissando** in double bass	▪ Bass habanera rhythm 3+3+2 quavers A–F–E ▪ **Additive rhythms** and **cross rhythms** ▪ Falling profile of melody (E–A) ▪ **Semitonal auxiliaries** including moving the top note earlier in the repeat ▪ Chromatically altering melody to fit chord – D♯/augmented 2nd interval ▪ **Circle of fifths** ▪ Unexpected chords – e.g. Fm exploring flat side harmony ▪ String techniques ▪ Move from Am to B♭m to Bm – semitone rise/raise temperature

Born in Argentina in 1921, Piazzolla reworked ideas found in Argentine tango to create a contemporary aspect of the form. By fusing the traditional form with more contemporary ideas found in jazz and twentieth-century classical music, he created a new type of tango – 'tango nuevo' – which he described by saying 'my tango does meet the present'. Two pieces that show these traditional and contemporary features are 'Milonga del Angel' and 'Yo soy Maria'.

'Milonga del Angel' combines the traditional and contemporary from the outset. Milonga is a significant word in tango, linking to an event or place where tango is danced as well as a type of music which is often of fast tempo in $\frac{2}{4}$ time. Piazzolla reworks this tradition by writing a slow tempo piece in $\frac{4}{4}$. The piece is in ternary form with a short introduction, with Piazzolla's traditional free approach to tonal scheme. While the introduction and opening A section are based around the tonic B minor, the B section modulates more widely including moves to Em, F#m and Cm – the flattened second degree. The repeat of the A section moves even further away from the tonic, traversing through C#m and Fm.

Further evidence of traditional tango can be found in Piazzolla's rhythmic choices. He employs the traditional habanera rhythm and shape in the bass (outlining tonic and dominant using a dotted rhythm and octave jump on beats 3 and 4) as well as syncopation. His choice of instruments – solo violin and bandoneon with accompaniment – is also traditional, with some more contemporary touches including vibrato on the bandoneon bellows, glissando on the bass and exploiting the full range of the violin in its countermelody – sul G, pitch bends creating expressive sus2 chords, and very high registers to contrast on the repeat.

Task 1: Completing 'Yo Soy Maria'

Now consider writing the second half of the essay to reference 'Yo soy Maria', using the indicative content outline above. This will give you detailed discussion on one of the named artists to answer the essay question.

Task 2: Adding a second artist

With the first named artist task now complete, plan the second half of the essay, referencing one or two pieces of music by one of the remaining named artists. Remember to give musical detail in your response, linking to the essay question.

When you have make this plan, write your paragraphs, as above. Finally, add to the introduction and write a conclusion to finish your work.

AoS6 KEY TERMS: A SUMMARY

Melody: raga, pitch bend, kumbengo (ostinato riffs on kora), birmintingo (improvised runs)

Harmony: drone, sus4 chords, chord symbols, added note chords

Tonality: specific modes

Structure: tango nuevo, milonga, fado, alap, fusion, verse/chorus, folk rock, song form/standard form

Sonority/Timbre: specific instruments, specific string techniques, studio effects, piano glissando, drone, sitar sympathetic strings

Texture: looping, layering, heterophonic

Tempo, metre and rhythm: polyrhythm, Latin 3+3+2 rhythm (additive), habanera rhythm, tala, riff

Art music since 1910

Introduction

The music of this Area of Study is some of the most moving and engaging music offered for study in the course.

There are four named artists in this AoS for you to listen to, study and gain a critical appreciation of. The specification cites that music in this genre is defined as 'music that comprises modern, contemporary classical, electronic art, experimental and minimalist music as well as other forms'.

- Dmitri Shostakovich
- Olivier Messiaen
- Steve Reich
- James MacMillan

Many of the musical terms listed in the specification are covered in other AoS, so it is advisable for you to work through the exercises in the previous chapters to help improve your knowledge.

The AQA A Level Music specification can be found at www.aqa.org. uk/subjects/music/as-and-a-level/music-7272. This contains a full list of the relevant vocabulary for each AoS. Further examples and explanations can be found in the AQA *AS and A Level Music Study Guide* (Rhinegold Education).

Initial aural analysis

Using the aural analysis table found on page 83, listen to the following piece to gain insight into how the musical elements are used. Check your responses against the information given in the Answers section at the back of the book.

MacMillan, *The Gallant Weaver*

You can find this piece here: http://bit.ly/TheGallantWeaver

Record your findings in a way that allows you to make additions and form links between the elements of music.

If you find that this way of working is a positive experience, consider doing this for other named artists. It can be an especially useful way of working where scores are not available.

Extended analysis

One of the exciting aspects of this AoS is the ability to give really detailed musical analysis, linking the music to its socio-political context.

The example below references the first movement of Shostakovich's Fifth Symphony; similar examples can be completed for the other named artists.

To what extent is this movement in sonata form?

While this is an unlikely direct examination question, it is a very useful angle to take to make an advanced argument in an analytical essay. Listen to the movement and consider the argument below:

Yes – it is in sonata form	No – it is not in sonata form
■ Clear **Exposition** involving first and second subject areas, defined by contrasting tonal areas (1 = Dm, 2 = E♭ minor) ■ **Development** section (fig.17–36) develops ideas heard earlier including tonal changes, rhythmic augmentation and dominant preparation on A ■ **Recapitulation** (from fig.36) returns to tonic D minor with second subject in tonic major (fig.39)	■ Tonal relationship of Dm/E♭m very **strained** – link to phrygian mode ■ Exposition is **developmental** ■ Development and Recapitulation are **blurred** – fig.36 feels like a climax to the development ■ Recapitulation does not use memorable material from first subject, instead using **subsidiary material** ■ When the first subject does appear it is **inverted** in a low flute in E minor played in a piano dynamic

Task 1: Essay

Write an essay using this material to argue whether or not the movement is in sonata form. Remember to include relevant musical detail to support your argument.

Task 2: Extension

Having completed this analysis for the first movement, look at the fourth movement of the symphony. Similar arguments can be applied here to suggest Shostakovich's outwardly conformist, inwardly rebellious approach to writing in sonata form.

	Exposition	Development	Recapitulation
Suggests sonata form	First subject = D minor Second subject = A major fig.110	Based on first and second subject material from fig.111	First subject from fig.121 First subject in tonic major from fig.131 – fanfare celebration
Questions sonata form	Second subject appears in F major (fig.108) under chaos semiquavers	Soon breaks out into new material from fig.113	The second subject does not appear in the Recapitulation – the very point of sonata form is undermined

Comparing named artists

The essay question in Section C is likely to ask you to compare two named artists, discussing how they have responded to different situations. As such, comparing similar genres is a very useful revision exercise.

This could be done for a large work such as a symphony, or a smaller piece of chamber music like the string quartet. The example below looks at how different named artists have approached writing for chamber ensembles.

Messiaen: Quartet for the End of Time (movement 2)

You can find this movement here: http://bit.ly/MessiaenQuatuor

- **Structure:** ABA Ternary – rhythmic and textural contrasts
- **Sonority/Timbre:** unusual combination of violin, clarinet, cello and piano, extremes of register, use of mutes and quiet dynamics
- **Rhythm:** frequent tempo changes before settling on slow $\frac{3}{4}$ time in B section, rhythmic variety, cells, syncopation, use of trill – link to birdsong
- **Melody:** modes of limited transposition, inversion, sequence, chant-like in B section
- **Texture:** doubling of melody at octave or double octave, 4-, 6- or 8-note chords; tessituras change, impacting texture
- **Harmony and Tonality:** verticalisation of the mode, chords on superimposed 4ths, parallelism, 'blue-orange' chords

Shostakovich: String Quartet No. 8 (movement 2)

You can find this movement here: http://bit.ly/ShostakovichQuartet8

- **Structure:** overall binary form with repetition ABA'B'
- **Sonority/Timbre:** violent use of string quartet, including *sff* double stopping, extreme range and advanced string crossing techniques
- **Rhythm:** exceptionally fast tempo giving one-in-a-bar feel; frequent syncopation and cross rhythms including accompaniment triplets in C section
- **Melody:** use of DSCH motif, chromatic, often conjunct with narrow, scurrying range, reuse of material from other works – autobiographical?
- **Texture:** solo plus aggressive chord accompaniment, use of octaves and double octaves
- **Harmony and Tonality:** G♯m and Cm with the movement suddenly ending on a repeated diminished chord built on a C♯

Macmillan: Memento for String Quartet

You can find this piece here: http://bit.ly/Memento1994

- **Structure:** through composed, free, fitting for purpose of piece
- **Sonority/Timbre:** high tessitura exploited with use of harmonics – still, fragile; glissando used gives emotive effect
- **Rhythm:** slow, expressive tempo, no clear pulse
- **Melody:** Gaelic lament themes emerge and vanish into silence, imitation
- **Texture:** use of silence to create structural division
- **Harmony and Tonality:** pedal points, expressive unresolved dissonance, minor mode exploited within the Gaelic lament tradition

Task: Symphonic comparison

Now complete a similar analytical comparison looking at larger-scale symphonic works by two of the named artists. As this form is significantly larger than chamber music, it is advisable to select detailed passages from a movement rather than try to cover all points.

Listening (Section A)

Track 1 – Shostakovich, *Jazz Suite No. 2*, Waltz

Listen to this piece which you can find here: http://bit.ly/JazzSuiteWaltz2

Extract: 0:00–0:30

1. Which two pitches are played by the bass from the opening of the extract? [2 marks]

2. What is the melodic compass of the saxophone in the first eight bars of its melody? Underline one answer.

   Perfect 4th **Perfect 5th** **Minor 6th** **Minor 7th** [1 mark]

3. Which one of these devices is used in this extract? Underline one answer.

   Chromatic Lower Appoggiatura **Chromatic Upper Appoggiatura**

   Chromatic Lower Auxiliary **Chromatic Upper Auxiliary** [1 mark]

   [Total: 4 marks]

Track 2 - Reich, *Electric Counterpoint,* Slow

Listen to this piece which you can find here: http://bit.ly/ElectricCounterpoint2

Extract: 0:00–0:45

1. Which instrument can be heard in this extract?   [1 mark]

2. Which two of the following are used in this recording?
   Underline two answers.

   Layering   **Phase Shifting**   **Metamorphosis**

   Note Addition   **Multitrack Recording**   [2 marks]

3. Which interval is used prominently in the opening cell?   [1 mark]

                                             [Total: 4 marks]

Track 3 - Messiaen, 'Louange à l'Éternité de Jésus'

Listen to this piece which you can find here: http://bit.ly/MessiaenQuatuor

Extract: 18:00–19:06

1. What instrument plays the solo melodic line?   [1 mark]

2. Which graphic score best represents the melodic contour
   of the opening melodic line?

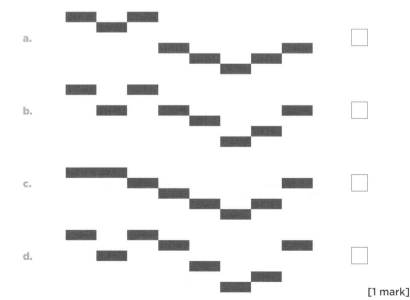

a.

b.

c.

d.

                                                 [1 mark]

3. What is the interval played by the solo instrument between the
   end of the first phrase and the return to the opening material?   [1 mark]

4. Underline the statement which is true.

   a. The piano plays only minor chords

   b. The piano plays only major chords

   c. The piano plays a mixture of major and minor chords

   d. The piano plays chords including diminished 7th chords   [1 mark]

[Total: 4 marks]

Track 4 – Messiaen, 'La Nativité'

Listen to this piece which you can find here: http://bit.ly/Messiaen1935

Extract: 0:00–2:08

The excerpt is called 'Jésus accepte la souffrance (Jesus accepts
suffering)' by Olivier Messiaen. It tells the story of how Jesus accepted
the fate destined for him by being born as man on earth.

How are the elements of music used to evoke this title?   [10 marks]

Essay question (Section C)

How has the approach of one of the named artists changed during this period? Discuss with reference to at least two contrasting pieces.

This question is looking at how the musical style of one of the artists has
changed over a period of time. It is an excellent question to approach for
revision for each of the named artists.

As you tackle this essay, remember the guidance given in the previous
chapters which have discussed approaches to writing the essay as well
as looking at how to style your work. The examples below show how this
essay might be written if the music of Shostakovich was being used.

Indicative content: Dmitri Shostakovich

1. Symphony No. 5 in D minor (1937)

Any of the four movements could be used as a starting point here, with the first and fourth movements being particularly useful in being able to discuss Shostakovich's approach to writing in sonata form. Use the information from earlier in this chapter to help you plan your thoughts.

2. Piano Concerto No. 2 (1957)

The playful character of the outer movements can offer a great contrast, showing a lighter more jovial quality, whilst the slow second movement can be directly compared to the slow movement of the Fifth Symphony.

3. Waltz from *Jazz Suite* (1938)

While the jazz influences are referenced rather than being central to this music, this work offers another diverse piece to show how Shostakovich's musical style has changed over time.

4. String Quartet No. 8 (1960)

The first and second movements of this autobiographical work have great expressive control and can be used to show how Shostakovich's writing changed over time. The information from earlier in this chapter can be used to discuss the second movement.

Over to you

The three paragraphs below each act as an introduction to a different piece by Shostakovich. Read each, marking the context. Create a rank order. What can we learn from these passages? What should we avoid?

1. Symphony No. 5, movement 4

Shostakovich wrote his Fifth Symphony in 1937 when he was under a lot of pressure from Stalin and the Soviet authorities to conform to their ideal of art. He was fearful for his life and managed to write a piece of music which appeased the authorities whilst also speaking to the Russian people. The fourth movement is written in sonata form with a clear exposition, development and recapitulation. The ending in D major brings a triumphant close to the music.

2. String Quartet No. 8, movement 1

Writing in an autobiographical nature, Shostakovich created a string quartet to be remembered by having joined the Communist Party in 1960. This movement is lonely and expansive, using the D – Eb – C – B motif in fugal treatment, outlining the composer's initials. The movement is full of quotation – bar 16 referencing his First Symphony and bar 55 using the first subject from the first movement of the Fifth Symphony – now transposed to A minor but retaining the phrygian semitone descent. It is structured in an arch form (ABCB'A') and makes extensive use of pedal points and chromatic, meandering melodic lines.

3. Waltz from *Jazz Suite*

The waltz genre is captured from the outset with a tonic – dominant ostinato and accompanying chords on the second and third beats of the bar. A saxophone melody, hinting at the jazz world, uses regular four-bar classical phrasing complete with some unexpected twists – notice the chromatic appoggiatura resolving from F# – G. The ternary form allows for a re-orchestration to occur in the reprise, with the trombone taking over from the saxophone, making use of its characteristic slide.

Essay task

Now write the essay yourself, writing about a named artist of your choice and being sure to include at least two contrasting pieces. Remember all the essay points covered so far in this revision guide to help you get the right balance between context, analysis and musical example.

AoS7 KEY TERMS: A SUMMARY

Melody: modes of limited transposition, whole tone scale, octatonic scale, pentatonic scale, hexatonic scale, tone row, note addition/subtraction, resultant melody, cells, motif, metamorphosis

Harmony: non-functional harmony, chord extensions, cluster chords, static harmony, open 5th harmony

Tonality: bitonality, tonal ambiguity, atonality, modality

Structure: cyclical structures, ostinato, cadenza

Sonority/Timbre: organ stops (reeds, mixture, swell pedal, tremulant), studio effects (reverb, sampling), unusual instruments (e.g. ondes Martenot), string effects (col legno, harmonics)

Texture: looping, layering, drone, a cappella

Tempo, metre and rhythm: additive rhythm, palindromic rhythm, metrical displacement, phasing, augmentation, diminution

Performance and composition: coursework components

As well as the final Appraising Music (Component 1) examination, you must also complete two coursework units, in Performance (Component 2) and Composition (Component 3).

Performance

This unit is worth 35% of the total marks at A Level; regular practice, keen research into your music and a willingness to listen to constructive criticism are all key attributes to producing a successful recital.

PERFORMING REQUIREMENTS

Minimum duration: 10 minutes

Options:

- Acoustic performance – solo and/or ensemble; instrumental and/or vocal

OR

- IT Production – presented to AQA in the form of a recording with a score, lead sheet or guide recording (if the former is unavailable).

Remember to ensure that your instrumental teacher is fully up to speed with the requirements for the unit; it has its own marking criteria which need to be fully understood to access the highest marks.

While planning your final recital is important, it is not the only performance-based activity you should be doing during the course. Consider playing through your composition work to establish if ideas are idiomatic and full of musical character. Also try out on your instrument the ideas you learn through your musical analysis.

Composition

This unit is worth 25% of the marks at A Level. You will be awarded for creative use of the musical elements, showing a strong musical technique and a keen awareness of musical development.

COMPOSING REQUIREMENTS

You must complete two separate compositions:

- Composition 1: composition to a brief set by AQA
- Composition 2: free composition

Combined, your compositions should last a minimum of 4½ minutes; any submissions falling below this minimum time will not be awarded any marks.

In-depth advice on the Performing and Composing tasks is available in the *AQA AS and A Level Music Study Guide* (Rhinegold Education).

Answers

AoS1 : Western Classical tradition 1650–1910

Pages 9–10: Exercise 1 – Contours

Description	Bar number(s)
An ascending scalic contour	1
A descending scalic contour	7
An ascending arpeggio contour	2
A descending arpeggio contour	8
A triadic contour	5
A conjunct (non-scalic) contour	3–4
A disjunct contour	6

Pages 10–11: Exercise 2 – Special melodic notes

Position (bar/beat)	Note name	Description
1^2	C	Unaccented passing note
1^3	A	Lower auxiliary
4^1	A	Appoggiatura
4^2	F	Accented passing note
5^1	C♯	Chromatic accented passing note

6¹	A	Lower auxiliary
7¹	F♯	Chromatic lower auxiliary
11³	D	Echappée
12¹	A	Unaccented passing note
12³	B♭	Note of anticipation

Page 11: Exercise 3 – Intervals

Bar	Notes	Interval
2	D – G	Perfect 4th
3	D – B♭	Minor 6th
3–4	F – A	Major 3rd
11	E♭ – C	Minor 3rd
11	F – E♭	Minor 7th
13	E♭ – A	Diminished 5th

Pages 12–14: Exercise 4 – Melodic devices

1. Two balanced 5-bar phrases
2. Motif
3. A lower chromatic auxiliary note
4. Intervallic augmentation
5. Rising sequence
6. Intervallic diminution and inversion
7. Fragmentation
8. Arpeggio
9. Falling by a 3rd
10. Repetition

Pages 14–15: Exercise 5 – Ornamentation

Ornament symbol	Ornament name	How played
A	Acciaccatura	E
B	Appoggiatura	D
C	Trill	B
D	Inverted Mordent	C
E	Mordent	F
F	Turn	A

Page 16: Exercise 6 – Diatonic chords and inversions

I   IV   ii   V   V7d   Ib   vi   ii   iib   iii

vi   iib   ii   Ic   V   Ib   IV   ii7b   Ic   V7   I

Pages 16–18: Exercise 7 – Cadences

Bar	Key	Chords	Cadence
2	G major	IV – I	Plagal
4	G major	Ic – V	Imperfect: half close
6	A minor	ic – V^7 – i	Perfect
8	G major	Ic – V^7 – I	Perfect
10	E minor	ii – V	Imperfect
12	E minor	ivb – V	Imperfect: phrygian
14	G major	iib – V	Imperfect
16	B minor	i – V	Imperfect
18	G major	iib – V^7 – vi	Interrupted
20	G major	V – I	Perfect (NB 4–3 suspension on V)

Pages 18–20: Exercise 8 – Advanced chords

Chord	Chord analysis
Bar 3^2	Augmented 6th (French)
Bar 5^1	Diminished 7th
Bar 5^2	Secondary dominant 7th (V^{7}b of IV)
Bar 7^2	Secondary dominant 7th (V^7 of V)
Bar 9^2	Secondary dominant 7th (V^7 of III)
Bar 11	Minor chord iv in C major

Bar 13[2]	Augmented 6th (initially Italian, then German)
Bar 18	Neapolitan 6th
Bar 19[1]	Diminished 7th
Bar 22	Chord I (Tierce de Picardie)

Page 20: Exercise 9 – Keys: signatures and relationships

1. 5
2. 4
3. C minor
4. A major
5. C minor
6. E major
7. B♭ minor
8. E minor
9. E♭ minor
10. E♭ major

Pages 20–21: Texture words

Texture term	Definition
Monophonic	One instrument or voice playing a single melodic line
Unison	Two or more instruments or voices playing the same melodic line at the same octave
Octaves texture	Two or more instruments or voices playing the same melodic line at two or more different octaves
Parallel 3rds	The same melodic line doubled at the interval of a 3rd

Melody and accompaniment	A distinct melodic line supported by a non-melodic accompaniment
Homophonic	Chordal music
Polyphonic	Two or more different melodic lines heard together (usually in choral music)
Contrapuntal	Two or more different melodic lines heard together (usually in instrumental music)
Fugal	Polyphonic or contrapuntal music which is based on a main melodic theme (the subject) which is heard alternately through each voice
Canonic	Polyphonic or contrapuntal music in which once voice has the same melodic line as another but starting later, and possibly from a different pitch
Antiphonal	Alternation in the texture between two groups of players / singers or registers

Pages 23-25: Question 1 - Baroque

1. Octave
2. Octaves texture
3. Minor
4. Circle of 5ths harmony
5. Bassoon
6. b
7. Relative major (B♭ major)
8. Subdominant (C minor)
9. 3 bars
10. Tonic pedal note
11. Relative of the subdominant
12. c

Pages 25–28: Question 1 – Classical

1. Bass
2. $\frac{3}{4}$
3. Adagio
4. Dominant
5. Triadic
6. Minor 7th
7. Ic – V⁷ – I
8. Homophony
9. Secondary 7th
10. 5 and 11
11. c
12. d

Pages 28–30: Question 1 – Romantic

1. b
2. a. 8, b. 6
3.

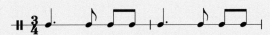

4. 6th
5. V⁷
6. Tonic pedal
7. IVc
8. vi
9. Perfect cadence in iii
10. Rising sequence
11. Secondary dominant 7th
12. Triplet quaver

Pages 34–39: Sample question 22

1. Augmented 4th [1 mark]
2. Circle of 5ths [1 mark]
3. ▪ At the start of the movement the ripieno instruments are playing the main ritornello themes in octave texture (bars 1–13)

- The ripieno is then silent for the first appearance of the solo flute (bars 13–20)
- The ripieno play an abbreviated ritornello in bars 21–26
- In bars 28–31 the violins of the ripieno add their own birdsong-like chirpings as accompaniment to the solo flute. For this they play in parallel 3rds
- From bar 32 Vivaldi uses the violas as a bass instrument – an unusual choice
- After bar 40, there is a more elaborate texture in the ripieno, with a contrapuntal relationship between the solo flute and the violins. The 1st violins play the trill-like semiquaver pattern under the flute's leaping dotted rhythm idea, and then the 2nd violins double the flute's conjunct semiquavers a 3rd below. This pattern is sustained as a sequence.
- The extract ends with the ripieno once again playing the ritornello theme, now in B minor [5 marks]

4. Answers should discuss contrasts of:
   - Scoring (tutti sections v. solo passages with basso continuo)
   - Melodic material (ritornello v. solo figurations)
   - Texture (monophonic, octaves, melody and accompaniment, parallel 3rds)
   - Tonality

   ...and give precise locations for examples that support the argument.
   [10 marks]

   [Total: 17 marks]

Pages 40–46: Sample question 23

1. Conjunct [1 mark]
2. Diminished 5th [1 mark]
3.
   - The first subject idea (bars 1–12) which represents Figaro is mainly accompanied by the strings
   - The non-stop semiquavers in the 2nd violins suggest the busy and excited atmosphere as Figaro and Susanna are getting ready for their wedding
   - The second subject (bars 12–17) which represents Susanna is largely accompanied by the winds
   - Interjections of semiquavers and staccato triplets from the violins in octaves (e.g. bar 14) suggest carefree happiness and laughter
   - From bar 19, with both characters involved, the orchestra is used in more intricate combinations

- The moment where Susanna finally gets Figaro's attention (bar 30) – the end of the transition – is marked by a full *tutti*
- Figaro now sings 'Susanna's tune' accompanied with his 'team' (the strings) much to the delight of Susanna, heard by the laughing flurry of semiquavers in her 'team' (the winds) [5 marks]

4. The music begins in G major with a '1st subject' for Figaro which has an assertive character with simple marching rhythm using repeating crotchets and confident leaps in the contour.

Whilst still in G major, Susanna enters with a contrasting melodic idea of graceful conjunct quavers, several of which act as appoggiaturas and often slurred pairs of notes to one syllable. The initial direction of the contour is downward. Figaro continues with his leaping interjections. Eventually this passage works as a transition, moving the music to the dominant key.

The '2nd subject' is then heard at bar 33 in D major. Significantly it takes the form of Figaro singing Susanna's tune: she has captured her fiancé's attention. The music in bar 38–42 acts as a codetta with repeated perfect cadences in the dominant. [10 marks]

[Total: 17 marks]

Pages 46–48: Sample question 24

1. Augmented [1 mark]
2. (Descending) sequence [1 mark]
3.
   - The subtlety of the ties in the accompanying pattern from bar 1 onwards
   - Melodic duplet against accompaniment triplets, e.g. bar 5
   - Semiquavers quickening into nontuplet semiquavers, e.g. bar 15
   - The quicker harmonic rhythm that comes with the change of metre in $\frac{6}{8}$ at bar 21
   - The hemiola-like rhythm (repeating pattern of four semiquavers) in bars 29-30 [5 marks]
4.
   - The melody is always at the top of the texture, with a soft mid-register harmonic accompaniment and occasional bass notes
   - Chromaticism is a significant factor in the harmonic palette, starting with the descending line in the LH in bars 1-2
   - Advanced chords include:
     - dominant 9th (3rd inversion) in bar 5, enhanced by lower chromatic auxiliary
     - half diminished 7th in bar 6 with rising chromatic appoggiatura on the downbeat

- a Neapolitan 6th (relating to previous D⁷ chord) in bar 10
- secondary dominant 7th (V⁷c of ii) in bar 12
- the dominant 13th in bar 13 (appropriately enough!)
- The B section from bar 15 explores the piano's registers with an upper register passage articulated by lower notes (via hand-crossing) in bars 17 and 20
- The texture from bar 21 is extremely pianistic and plays to the sonority of a concert grand piano with a two-part RH texture and wide-ranging LH arpeggios, enhanced by use of the sustaining pedal
- This builds to a climactic wash of sound in bars 29-32 [10 marks]

[Total: 17 marks]

AoS2: Pop music

Page 57: Harmonic analysis

G⁷/B   C   C⁷/E   D   C♯dim   Dsus4   B⁷/D♯   Em

Page 60: Muse, 'Mercy'

1. 4 (C, G, Em, Dsus4)
2. Final quaver in bass before voice starts (C♯), which is the sharpened 4th in G major
3. Minor 7th (C – D)

Page 61: Track 1 – Joni Mitchell, 'Blue'

1. Quavers [1 mark]
2. One chord every bar [1 mark]
3. Melisma [1 mark]
4. 9th (B – A) [1 mark]

Pages 61–62: Track 2 – Daft Punk, 'Instant Crush'

1. a [1 mark]
2. d [1 mark]
3. Syllabic [1 mark], exact musical repetition [1 mark] with changed lyrics [1 mark] [max 2 marks]

Page 62: Track 3 – Beyoncé, 'Ave Maria'

Award marks according to the following band descriptions:

9–10	A comprehensive and authoritative response which is consistently coherent and logically structured
7–8	A wide-ranging and confident response which is mostly coherent and well structured
5–6	A relevant response despite some inaccuracy/omission and weaknesses in terms of coherency and structure
3–4	A limited response with some significant inaccuracy/ omission and a lack of clarity
1–2	A rudimentary response
0	No work submitted or worthy of credit.

Reference could be made to:

- Broken chord accompaniment using diatonic major keys including C major, C major 7 (added minor 7th/B♭), second inversion chords, chromatic alteration of the subdominant (F major to F minor), use of tonic pedal in bass
- Use of piano, guitar and later strings in lower register, complete with gentle percussion on beats 2 and 4 to give a chilled and relaxed effect
- Slow tempo (crotchet = 75) in compound time ($\frac{12}{8}$) – accept $\frac{4}{4}$ use of triplets
- Conjunct melodic lines in hushed lower register
- Use of more operatic sound quality at 'Ave Maria' to link to classical tradition
- Repetition between verses and choruses
- Any other valid points

Pages 63-66: Essay question (Section C)

Named Artist 1: Stevie Wonder 'Superstition' (1972)

Named Artist 2: Labrinth 'Beneath your beautiful' (2012),
'Let the Sun Shine' (2010) [1]

'Superstition' by Stevie Wonder is a famous funk-inspired
piece with an opening bass riff which is iconic. [2] *The key*
characteristics of funk include a complex groove,
interjections from the horn section and interlocking drum
patterns and many of these features can be found in the
piece. [3] *It uses the Eb minor pentatonic scale with four*
straight quavers followed by a more complex second part of
the bar. The second [4] *clavinet part plays an Eb major 7*
chord underneath this 2-bar riff, giving an Ebb7#9 chord
with the major and minor third played simultaneously. [5]
The bass guitar anchors the riff, playing on the beat Ebs
before increased quaver movement in the final two beats
of the bar. Wonder's vocals also employ the Ebm pentatonic
scale with subtle syncopation over this accompaniment,
dovetailing with the three-layered texture.

While the riff itself is memorable and central to the song,
it is by no means the only factor in the success of the piece.
The piece develops in three main ways. Firstly, Wonder
introduces a horn riff (tenor saxophone and trumpet) at
'thirteen month old baby'. [6] *This new riff has an ascending*
profile using semiquavers, again employing the pentatonic
scale, peaking on a top Bb. The use of ties aids the
syncopation. A second development occurs in the short
chorus, where the harmonic rhythm changes to two chords
per bar, outlining V7, bvi7 and V7 secondary dominant
(V7b of V) in minims before settling on IV7 for a whole
bar, eventually resolving to a crotchet V+ augmented
triad on Bb. [7] *This chromatic chord allows for a one-bar*
breakdown to interrupt the flow of the music. [8]
Finally, a 4-bar link with the horn section prominently
using C natural [9] *in a contrasting descending pattern leads*
into the bridge which repeats the chorus chords complete
with a vocal 'howl'. This allows the music to achieve a sense
of repetition and change, sustaining musical character.

Many successful pop songs do not make [10] *use of*
memorable riff patterns, with Labrinth's 'Beneath Your
Beautiful' being one such song. The 4-bar introduction

[1] This list approach is a quick way of telling the examiner which pieces you will use to answer the question

[2] Directly links to question

[3] Context is good especially when it is directly linked to the question and the set work being discussed.

[4] What does the first clavinet do?

[5] Is this new? Or old? Link to Jazz?

[6] Direct reference to the piece - specific

[7] Mention use of sextuplet as a new rhythmic idea in combination with this chromatic chord?

[8] This could be expanded

[9] Why is this so important given the music heard up to this point?

[10] This argues the other side of the essay = balance

uses repeated constant quavers in the piano right hand with an ascending 2-bar pattern in the left. The chords are anchored on D (the tonic) and A (the dominant) though there is some gentle dissonance to help give the ballad feeling – such as the G major 7 chord in bar 2. The verse is reliant on a repeating 2-bar chord sequence of D Em G A with the piano playing block chords, allowing the vocals (complete with gentle syncopation) to have the musical focus. Interestingly, the chorus (from 'would you let me') uses the same chord pattern as the verse with a few small developments, including adding a 7th to the Em chord, 9th to the G major chord and at the line 'take it off now' adding a new B minor chord. Later in the song Emeli Sandé joins Labrinth's vocals, with both singing in <u>3rds</u> [11] to develop the musical texture. <u>The song ends with a repetition of the opening.</u> [12]

'Let the Sun Shine', another Labrinth single released in 2010, is another successful song which makes use of a riff in a <u>different way.</u> [13] Here, the rhythmic groove is relaxed with a tempo of crotchet = 110 which is animated by use of a semiquaver riff played on one high note on a synthesizer. This figure uses semiquaver rests (on the 4th, 9th and 16th semiquaver beats) as well as one quaver on the 11/12th beats to add musical excitement to the song. However, the riff is not the main musical focus here with the vocals having dominance. The chord progression, like in 'Beneath your Beautiful', is a simple repetitive cycle of Em C and G, with the bridge having greater harmonic venture including a flatwise modulation to Eb, Cm7, F and Bb. The bass, using dotted rhythms, is also simple in construction, being used from the first chorus onwards. <u>It is the combination of these elements which allows for the success of the song, not the riff alone.</u> [14]

While the use of riff remains an important part of pop song composition, it is by no means the only aspect required to create a successful piece of pop music. Popular music which gains fame makes use of a combination of elements – memorable melodic lines, pleasing chord progressions, development of ideas and use of riff – to create a piece which is musically satisfying.

Mark: probably high 19–24 band

[11] Example?

[12] A final sentence linking to the question is needed here to keep the essay on track.

[13] Good to have a third line of argument.

[14] Good summary sentence, linking to the question

AoS3: Music for media

Page 69: Harmonic analysis

B♭   B♭7/D   E♭sus4   E♭7 A♭ F7/A B♭sus4   F   D7/F♯ Gsus2   F7   B♭

Page 69: Complex chords

Given the nature of this AoS you should be able to find many examples of these chords.

Chord	Symbol	Notation	Example
Augmented triad C – E – G♯	C+		Herrmann – *Psycho 'Prelude'*
Added 6th chord	C6		
Diminished triad	C°		
Diminished 7th	C7o		
Half diminished 7th	Cø		

Page 72: Track 1 – Herrmann, *Vertigo* 'Main Theme'

1. $\frac{6}{8}$ [1 mark]

2. Minor 2nd/semitone [1 mark]

3. Ostinato [1 mark]

4. Contrary motion [1 mark]

Pages 72–73: Track 2 – Zimmer, *Angels and Demons* '160 bpm'

1. $\frac{7}{8}$ [1 mark]
2. Tonic pedal [1 mark]
3. b [1 mark]
4. Augmented 2nd (no marks for minor 3rd) [1 mark]

Page 73: Track 3 – Zimmer, *Pearl Harbor* 'War'

Award marks according to the band descriptions given in the box on page 134.

Reference could be made to:

- Driving tempo – fast, agitated $\frac{2}{2}$ time
- Use of tonic pedal in quavers (B)
- Ascending sequence in bass using quavers and crotchet rests
- Unexpected modulation from B minor to F major (tritone relationship)
- Majestic theme (idea of war being a heroic act) with ascending minim profile
- Suspensions – e.g. 4-3 though often using modal chord V
- Tempo changes to reflect changes of scene
- Syncopation, especially in bass
- Use of triplets – militaristic
- Accelerando
- Main theme/triumphant melody at close – C major, use of minims, military triplet drum beat

Any other valid points.

Pages 74–79: Essay question (Section C)

Comment on Candidate A:

This essay is heavy on non-musical description with the entire first paragraph – nearly a third of the essay – having no musical detail whatsoever.

When the musical analysis does start there is some acknowledgement of relevant issues, with D minor and the opening theme correctly identified. However, description soon comes again to the fore as the plot is described at the expense of musical detail. There are inaccuracies too – the male vocal line (F–E–F–G♯) is more than just semitones and the comment 'trills and crescendos add interest' does not qualify what is being made more interesting. G major is not the relative major of D minor. The language is colloquial and short on perceptive musical comment. The candidate also incorrectly suggests Herrmann as the named artist – it is of course Zimmer.

The second piece contains some detail but, by referencing Zimmer again (albeit briefly), technically does not answer the question which requires two contrasting named artists.

Mark: most likely low end of 7–12 band

Comment on Candidate B:

The introduction moves directly into addressing the question and using correct musical vocabulary, introducing both named artists. There is a clear essay style from the outset. The musical analysis shows a commanding grasp of relevant issues and assured musical understanding, with the aural experience being clear throughout. There is a high level of music analysis and description is mostly avoided in a mature writing style. The plot is not described without appropriate analytical detail. There is little mention of textural changes in either piece, though harmonic and melodic detail is often strong. Analysis of the Zimmer is stronger than that of the Herrmann. The conclusion is stylish, addressing the question.

Mark: most likely low end of 25–30 band

AoS4: Music for theatre

Pages 84–85: Study Piece 2: Weill, *Rise and Fall of the City of Mahagonny* 'Alabama Song'

1st playing	■ Sonority – male tenor, chorus (2-part), soprano, strings accompaniment, crotchet accompaniment on piano/guitar, strings, drums with brass countermelody; forces change on repeats
	■ Ambiguous – opening suggests minor with move to major when soprano sings
	■ $\frac{4}{4}$, moderato blues tempo
	■ Song form – verses (minor) and chorus (major)
2nd playing	■ Verse conjunct, fragmented; chorus more lyrical
	■ Accompaniment figure – crotchet ostinato figure (verse) developed to quaver-quaver-crotchet ostinato in chorus
	■ Some dissonance especially in verse
	■ Moves to G major for the chorus; verse suggests C minor

3rd playing	▪ Verse uses semitone pedal points (C and B) with chords changing every 4 bars; chorus has tonic pedal on G with harmonic changes in 4-bar chunks
	▪ Contrast of fragmented verses and 4-bar phrasing in chorus
	▪ Melody and accompaniment
	▪ 1930s recording – different quality experience to more modern processed recordings; ghostly effect of 'I tell you we must die' – chromatic, vocal tone
4th playing	▪ Confirm the verse/chorus structure, noting differences between them
	▪ Harmony – extended chord use (use of Cm11 chords) plus use of chromaticism – Fm^7 – C^{7+4} – F^7 pattern
	▪ Tonality – move between Cm and B major in verse – unrelated, link to lyrics
	▪ Any other valid points

Page 85: Track 1 – Rodgers, *The Sound of Music* 'Edelweiss'

1. V^7 (accept D major 7) [1 mark for V, 2 marks for V^7, 0 marks for 7]
2. Major [1 mark]
3. c [1 mark]

Page 86: Track 2 – Sondheim, *Into the Woods* 'Agony'

1. $\frac{6}{8}$ [1 mark]
2. Major 2nd [1 mark]
3. Perfect 5th [1 mark]
4. Flattened 7th (D natural in E major) [1 mark]

Page 86: Track 3 – Jason Robert Brown, *Songs for a New World* 'Christmas Lullaby'

Award marks according to the band descriptions given in the box on page 134.

Reference could be made to:

▪ High tessitura of piano – bell-like with bare 5th chords in left hand and inverted tonic pedal on C; chords move in parallel motion including to B♭ (just before vocals start)

▪ Simple $\frac{4}{4}$ time, moderate tempo, major tonality, ostinato figure

▪ Excited lyrics – use of syncopation, ties and triplets but within context

- Move to relative minor ('but in the eyes of heaven')
- Emotive use of major 6th interval
- Use of unrelated chords, e.g. D major replacing expected tonic chord, B♭ replacing expected dominant chord
- 'Gloria' loudest dynamic

Any other valid points.

Pages 87–89: Essay question (Section C)

The essay content is covered in the Study Guide and in this Revision Guide. Like all essays it should be marked to the assessment grid within the specification on the AQA website.

AoS5: Jazz

Page 93: Blues scales

Hexatonic Scale:

Heptatonic Scale:

Nonotonic Scale:

Page 97: Track 1 – Louis Armstrong, 'Nobody Knows'

1. 6th (major 6th) [1 mark]
2. Syllabic, Spread chord [2 marks]
3. Plagal (IV – I) [1 mark]

Page 97: Track 2 – Charlie Parker, 'Summertime'

1. Octave [1 mark]
2. Blues notes [1 mark]
3. Straight quavers (not swung) [1 mark]
4. Tremolo [1 mark]

Page 97: Track 3 – Miles Davis, 'All Blues'

Award marks according to the band descriptions given in the box on page 134.

Reference could be made to:

- The relatively slow tempo, with a feeling of 2 in a bar despite the $\frac{6}{4}$ time signature
- The lighter tone provided by the alto and tenor sax riff (in 3rds), piano double trill, use of brushes and bass riff, as well as trumpet mute
- The gradual working out of the trumpet melody, focusing on the interval of a 6th (D–B)
- Increased expressive potential of the music, e.g. by use of vibrato
- Use of modes as a basis of improvisation
- Use of the ride cymbal within solo passages
- Relatively simple harmonic palette: 12-bar blues using G with added 7th. Other chords including $D^{7\flat9}$ and $E\flat^{7\flat9}$ are also explored

Any other valid points.

Pages 98–100: Essay question (Section C)

The Miles Davis 'Four' work has some relevant information and is particularly strong on harmonic analysis. However, only the first few bars are really discussed, and while the harmonic analysis is correct it is a little descriptive in nature. There is little discussion on the melodic features of the music. Some attempt is made to explain the Bebop style, but this is again brief and prone to description.

The analysis of 'All Blues' is accurate and starts to make comparisons on style. Harmony is well detailed, with some examples, but melody is left rather unexplored.

Moving forwards, consider rewriting this to include more perceptive analysis, greater musical detail and further examples to help justify your response. Consider which artist you could use as a contrast, ensuring you use comparative language to address the question.

AoS6: Contemporary traditional music

Page 103: String techniques

Name	Evidence	Description
Chicharra	http://bit.ly/ Chicharra	'cricket' – using the heel of the bow to play on the cotton part of the D string of the violin to create a percussive, low pitch squeak
Latigo	http://bit.ly/ TangoLatigo	'whip' – played on the E string of the violin using a slow to fast bow coupled with a glissando up or down the string
Arrastre	http://bit.ly/ Arrastre	'to drag' – slow to fast bow acceleration into a downbeat; often used in the bass part
Tambor	http://bit.ly/ TangoTambor	'small drum' – placement of second finger against the G but finger on the D with accented pizzicato on the G string giving a percussive, dry sound
Golpe de Caja	http://bit.ly/ GalopeDeCaja	'hit the box' – striking the box of the string instrument using a hand, fingers, with or without rings, to create different percussive sounds

Pages 105–106: Indian raga and Anoushka Shankar

Traditional raga elements	Contemporary elements
▪ Use of raga ▪ Use of tihais (3 repetitions) ▪ Link between sitar and tabla player ▪ Fast gat section (fixed composition) ▪ Use of fast ascending and descending scalic passages	▪ Fusion of instruments – cello, vocals in English, hang drum ▪ Use of sitar but not playing traditional rag – rather scales and flourishes ▪ Verse-chorus structure

Page 107: Track 1 – Anoushka Shankar, 'Prayer in Passing'

1. Drone [1 mark]
2. Tremolo [1 mark]
3. Minor 2nd (D–E♭) [1 mark]
4. Sampling [1 mark]

Page 107: Track 2 – Mariza, 'Retrato'

1. $\frac{4}{4}$ [1 mark]
2. Tierce de Picardie [1 mark]
3. Cello [1 mark]
4. Dominant [1 mark]

Page 108: Track 3 – Piazzolla, 'Anxiety'

Award marks according to the band descriptions given in the box on page 134.

Reference could be made to:

- Use of syncopation, with accents on weak beats
- Chromatic alteration in opening bandoneon part, E–E♭–D–D♭–C, giving chromatic twists
- Accented dissonant chords from string quartet including use of tremolo and heavy accents on off beat
- Use of additive rhythms 3+3+2
- Viola solo (then to cello) with dissonant (F♯/G/B) chords on beats one and three from bandoneon
- Aggressive playing style suggests unease

Any other valid points.

Pages 108–111: Essay question (Section C)

This essay should be marked to the assessment criteria on the AQA website.

AoS7: Art music since 1910

Page 112: Aural analysis – MacMillan, *The Gallant Weaver*

Points of consideration could include:

- **Structure:** verse form: 1 and 3 are linked, 2 and 4 are linked. Verse 5 ('I love') is new material in the same idiom as opening verses, ending in hushed 'mmm' hummed notes

- **Sonority/Timbre:** SATB with extensive division, especially in soprano (opening three-part texture). ATB initially support the weaving melodic lines from the sopranos before becoming increasingly independent

- **Rhythm:** Gaelic flourishes abound with use of semiquaver/demisemiquaver motifs. The opening melody is treated in imitation between the parts – a feature which repeats later on

- **Melody:** use of imitation, doubling of voices to give a written-out reverberation effect, some use of nonsense syllables, psalmody suggested

- **Texture:** SSS at start, use of full choir often with counterpoint and imitation between parts

- **Harmony and Tonality:** verticalisation of the mode, chords on superimposed 4ths, parallelism, 'blue-orange' chords

Page 116: Track 1 – Shostakovich, *Jazz Suite No. 2,* Waltz

1. Tonic (I/C) and Dominant (V/G) [2 marks]
2. Minor 6th (C–A♭) [1 mark]
3. Chromatic Lower Appoggiatura [1 mark]

Page 117: Track 2 – Reich, *Electric Counterpoint*, Slow

1. Electric guitar [1 mark]
2. Multitrack Recording, Layering [2 marks]
3. 4th [1 mark]

Pages 117–118: Track 3 – Messiaen, 'Louange à l'Éternité de Jésus'

1. Cello [1 mark]
2. b [1 mark]
3. Octave [1 mark]
4. b [1 mark]

Page 118: Track 4 – Messiaen, 'La Nativité'

Award marks according to the band descriptions given in the box on page 134.
Reference could be made to:

- Arresting fortissimo dissonant chords resolving to an E minor triad, using 16/8/4 foot foundation stops plus reeds, sounding like a whip
- Four-note motif in the pedals, E G F B♭ (and then back to E), evoking the four sides of the cross
- This aggressive passage is divided by a quieter, more chromatic section using Unda Maris stop on the Choir manual and an increasingly sustained set of pedal notes and a lack of the use of the organ pedals
- New idea towards the close using dissonant chords played staccato on the manuals which gradually rise and slowly have extra notes added, increasing the rhythmic and harmonic tension
- Use of swell box to facilitate crescendo

Any other valid points.

Pages 118–120: Essay question (Section C)

The three paragraphs offer a short introduction to each of the pieces. Remember that context does not equal marks in a music essay.

The rank order, from best to worst, is likely to be:

String Quartet No.8

- There is lots of musical detail here and context is generally given without being at the expense of musical detail
- There is some analysis of the melodic material, including referencing back to the symphony from which it came

Jazz Suite Waltz

- Context is minimal here and there is some relevant musical detail
- However, the writing is prone to description over musical analysis, and more in-depth writing could be given to analyse the melodic contour
- Bar references could be given to help justify the points

Symphony No. 5

- There is some musical detail here (mention of sonata form and the D major close), but this often lacks detail or example
- The sonata form point could be challenged
- Context is overbearing in this response and prevents the candidate from analysing the music itself

Your completed essay should be marked to the assessment scheme on the AQA website.

Glossary

12-bar blues One of the most prominent chord progressions in popular music, starting in blues music and spreading to jazz, rock, R&B, etc.

32-bar song form A name sometimes used for **popular song form** when each phrase is eight bars long.

A cappella Unaccompanied singing; from the Italian meaning 'in the chapel style', this term originally applied to church music, but is now used in contemporary vocal music.

Acciaccatura An ornament printed as a small note with a slash through its tail, which is played as quickly as possible before the main note that follows it; also known as a grace note.

Additive rhythm A rhythm where the bar is divided into beats of unequal length, e.g. 3+3+2.

Alap The opening section of a piece of Indian classical music, usually with melodic improvisation and free rhythm, developing into a **raga**.

Anacrusis One or more weak-beat notes before the first strong beat of a phrase, which is often called a 'pick up' in pop music (plural: anacruses).

Antecedent and consequent phrases Used to describe a pairing of phrases, typically found in **periodic phrasing**. Alternatively, the second phrase may be called an answering phrase. The two phrases will match in length, usually in rhythm, and sometimes in contour.

Antiphony, antiphonal A musical texture where two groups of musicians take it in turns to play; can also refer to sections of alternating registers.

Appoggiatura A melodic ornament where a neighbouring note (that sounds dissonant) is sounded for a measured period of time before the main note of the melody. In the Romantic era appoggiaturas are also found in the accompanying harmonic texture.

Arco An instruction for string players to use the bow, after playing pizzicato.

Aria An extended vocal solo in an opera, oratorio or cantata.

Arpeggio The notes of a standard triad played one after another, in ascending or descending order, that is, the 1st, 3rd, 5th and 8th notes of a scale.

Arrastre From Spanish, meaning 'drag', a specialist bow stroke that changes the bow speed from slow to fast, usually onto the downbeat. Often heard in the double bass part of an **orquesta típica**.

Articulation How smoothly or otherwise the notes are played, e.g. very detached (**staccato**), or joined together (**legato**) are types of articulation.

Atonal, atonality Western music without an obvious home key. Atonal music avoids major and minor keys (and also **modes**).

Augmentation Literally means 'expanded'. The opposite of **diminution**. It can refer to various features:

- **Interval**: an augmented interval is a semitone wider than a major or perfect interval, e.g. C–D♯, C–F♯
- **Chord**: a triad made up of two major 3rds, e.g. C–E–G♯
- **Rhythm**: a proportionate increase in the note lengths of a melody, for example, when two quavers and a crotchet are augmented they become two crotchets and a minim.

Auxiliary note A melodic decoration and non-harmony note one step away from the chord onto which it resolves, creating **dissonance.** They can be higher or lower than the chord, and so described as upper or lower auxiliary notes respectively. Where an accidental is used to create an auxiliary note that is a semitone away from the harmony note, this is called a **chromatic auxiliary note**.

Backbeat A term used in pop music to describe accenting the normally weak second and fourth beats in $\frac{4}{4}$ time.

Bare 5ths A texture where a melodic line is simultaneously played (doubled) a 5th higher or lower, thus creating a sparse, hollow effect, sometimes reminiscent of medieval organum (a style associated with monastic singing): see also open 5ths.

Basso continuo The fundamental basis of most orchestral and ensemble music in the Baroque period, represented in the score by the bass line that includes **figured bass** notation. This is played by a bass instrument (typically a cello, possibly a bassoon or other options) and a harmony instrument (harpsichord, organ or lute).

Bebop A style of jazz developed in the 1940s, notable for fast tempos, complex harmonies, virtuosic playing and much use of improvisation.

Belt A style of singing sometimes found in music theatre and pop music in which the singer uses their chest voice (usually a low register sound) above its natural range with a very loud dynamic.

Binary form A musical structure of two sections each of which is repeated to give ‖: A :‖‖: B :‖. The A section usually modulates to the dominant (or relative major); the B section starts in the dominant (or relative major) and returns to the tonic. Sometimes the B section refers to the opening tune of the A section to mark the return to the tonic key; this is known as **rounded binary form**.

Birimintingo Improvised solo melodic runs in kora playing.

Blue note In blues music, notes used in the melodic line which do not belong to the fundamental major key of the music, e.g. a flattened 3rd or flattened 7th.

Break A short instrumental solo, often improvised, in pop and jazz.

Breakdown A section of a song where various instrumentalists all have solo **breaks**.

Bridge A contrasting section in a pop song which usually joins the verse to the chorus, or is heard after twice through the verse and chorus.

Broken chord A chord in which the notes are sounded individually, or spread, rather than all being played exactly together. An arpeggio is a type of broken chord.

Cadence A pair of chords which mark the end of a musical statement. See p16 for perfect, imperfect, plagal and interrupted cadences.

- **Half-close** A type of imperfect cadence, Ic-V
- **Phrygian** ivb-V in a minor key, where the bass line moves down a semitone and the top line moves up a tone; common in Baroque music, and another type of imperfect cadence
- **Cadential 6/4** A second inversion chord resolving to the dominant, so Ic-V, another type of imperfect cadence

Call and response Vocal music in which a soloist sings a phrase to which a group of singers respond. Found in African music, as well as in jazz and pop music.

Canon A contrapuntal device in which a melody in one part is repeated note for note in another part starting a few beats later (and possibly at a different pitch), while the melody in the first part continues to unfold.

Chalumeau register The lowest range of a clarinet, with a rich, dark tone.

Chicharra In tango music, a technique where the violinist plays the strings *behind* the bridge, with heavy downward pressure on the bow, to emulate the sound of a cicada or cricket.

Chorus In music technology, when two sounds with similar timbral qualities are placed together to sound as one.

Chromatic Notes that don't belong to the current key; the opposite of **diatonic.**

Circle of 5ths progression A series of chords whose roots are each a perfect 5th lower than the previous chord.

Cluster chord A chord of at least three adjacent notes (probably semitones).

Coda The final section of a composition; where following repeated sections, such as in **32-bar song form**, the coda will be different from earlier sections.

Codetta A coda to a section of music, e.g. in sonata form, the close of an exposition section before the development starts.

Colla voce Literally meaning 'with the voice', indicating a freer tempo for the soloist, and the accompanying instruments should follow.

Col legno Played with the wood of a bow, rather than the hair, producing a dry sound.

Compound interval Intervals which are greater than an octave, so compound 5th describes an octave (or even two octaves) plus a 5th.

Compound time A metre in which the main beat can be subdivided into three. Common time signatures are $\frac{6}{8}$, $\frac{12}{8}$, $\frac{6}{4}$. The opposite of **Simple time**.

Conjunct A style of melodic writing in which each note is a step away from the previous one.

Consonant (harmony) A combination of notes providing a pleasing sound when played together, the opposite of **dissonant**. This is generally achieved by avoiding notes that are a semitone, tone or tritone apart.

Con sordino Played with a mute on the instrument thereby altering the timbre (on bowed string instruments and brass instruments).

Contour As contours on a map indicate the ups and downs of a landscape, this term is used to describe the rise and fall (or shape) of a melody line, such as ascending, descending, scalic, arpeggio, conjunct, disjunct.

Contrapuntal Music that uses **counterpoint**, a texture where two or more melodic lines are played together at the same time.

Cool jazz A lighter style of jazz, with a laid-back style of relaxed tempos, contrasting with the earlier **bebop** style.

Countermelody An independent melody sounding against another melody which has already been heard.

Counterpoint The simultaneous combination of two or more melodies with independent rhythms. There may be some imitation between parts, but counterpoint can also be non-imitative. A whole movement may be contrapuntal, or the music may alternate between contrapuntal and other textures. This term is often used interchangeably with **polyphony,** but is more commonly used for instrumental music.

Cross-rhythm A pattern in which the rhythmic detail of the music is out of phase with the underlying pulse (as in a **hemiola**), or where different subdivisions of the beat are used simultaneously (as in duple and triplet quavers).

Delay Guitar device which records a sound and repeats it at a given time, or multiple times, often with a diminuendo. Not to be confused with an echo, which does not repeat the sound.

Diatonic Music using just the notes of the home key; the opposite of **chromatic**.

Diegetic music Music that is heard in a film, the source of which is part of the film, such as the band in the saloon, the busker on the street, the organ in the church.

Diminished chord A triad made up of two minor 3rds, e.g. C–E♭–G♭. A diminished 7th is made up of three minor 3rds.

Diminution Literally means 'reduced'. The opposite of **augmentation**. It can refer to various features:

- **Interval**: a diminished interval is a semitone narrower than a major or perfect interval, e.g. C–D♭, C–G♭

- **Chord**: a triad made up of two minor 3rds, e.g. C–E♭–G♭

- **Rhythm**: a proportionate reduction in the note lengths of a melody, for example, when two quavers and a crotchet are diminished they become two semiquavers and a quaver.

Disjunct A style of melodic writing including many leaps between one note and the next; opposite of **conjunct**.

Dissonant, dissonance A combination of notes producing a clashing sound when played together; opposite of **consonant.**

Distortion A technological effect used to alter the sound of an amplified instrument, usually creating a 'dirty' or 'clipped' version of the same sound.

Dominant 7th Literally the note that is a 7th above the dominant; however, it is usually used to describe the dominant chord when the 7th note is included. The result is very direction-inducing, usually requiring resolution onto the tonic chord.

Doubled, doubling More than one part playing the same line, either in unison or an octave apart. Doubling of a melody can also occur at other intervals, e.g. at a 3rd for a consonant effect, or at a 4th for a more spikey, aggressive effect.

Double stopping Two notes played at the same time on a stringed instrument on two adjacent strings.

Double time In jazz, an instruction to change to using notes of double speed (e.g. semiquavers instead of quavers) without changing the underlying tempo of the chord progression. Often used in improvised solos.

Drone One or more notes held or repeated throughout an extended passage of music. Some instruments, such as bagpipes and sitar, have an inbuilt drone.

Echappée note An unaccented, dissonant melodic decoration note, that is one step higher or lower than the essential note, and then resolves by a leap back to the harmony note.

Enharmonic Two notes or keys which sound the same but are written differently, such as C♯ and D♭.

Episode A solo passage occurring in a **ritornello** movement.

Extended chord A triad with notes added to it, such as a 7th, 9th, 11th or 13th.

Fado Portuguese traditional sung ballad.

False relation A simultaneous or adjacent occurrence in different parts of a note in its natural form and its sharpened or flattened form.

Fermata A pause on a note or a rest.

Fill In pop music, a mini instrumental solo between the phrases of a song; the term is usually used with the name of the instrument playing, e.g. drum fill.

Fioritura An embellishment to a melody line, often an improvisation by an opera singer.

Four-on-the-floor Bass drum of a drum kit, playing on every crotchet in a $\frac{4}{4}$ bar, common in disco music of the 1970s.

Fours In jazz, when the players in the band take turns performing solos or improvisations for four bars. Usually this keeps going back to the drummer, for instance in a piano trio: Piano > Drums > Bass > Drums > Piano, etc.

Foursquare A passage of four 4-bar phrases. It is a less sophisticated version of **periodic phrasing** where there is a clear hierarchy of 2-bar, 4-bar and 8-bar pairings.

Fragmentation A compositional technique of breaking down a theme into its constituent motifs and repeating and developing them.

French 6th An augmented chord containing the root, major 3rd, augmented 4th and augmented 6th.

Fugue, fugal A contrapuntal musical form in which a main theme is taken up and developed by each part in turn.

Functional harmony A term sometimes used to describe standard tonal harmony in which primary and secondary triads are used with a sense of hierarchy and direction, and chromatic inflexions are understood in terms of conventions such as **secondary dominant 7ths**.

German 6th An augmented 6th chord containing the root, major 3rd, perfect 5th and augmented 6th.

Ghost note In jazz, a note with a rhythmic value but no obvious pitch, notated with an 'x' in place of a note head.

Glissando A compositional technique requiring the pitch to slide from one note to another: see also **portamento**.

Golpe de Caja From Spanish, meaning 'hit on the box'. In tango, an instruction to string players to hit the box part of the instrument. This can be done in a variety of ways, such as thumb knuckles or palm, each creating a different sound. More likely on the double bass, but also possible on the violin.

Groove A jazz term for the rhythmic 'feel' of a piece of music.

Habanera rhythm Traditional dance rhythm of Cuban and South American music.

Hang drum A metal percussion instrument, with different tone fields providing different notes similar to steel pans, and played with the hands.

Hard bop A subgenre of jazz, developed from bebop, with hard, funky rhythms and blues influence.

Harmonic rhythm The rate at which the harmony changes in a piece of music.

Harmonic series On many instruments these are the notes which occur 'naturally', due to the way a string vibrates or the air vibrates in a brass instrument to create certain pitches.

Harmonics On string instruments, including harp and guitar, a very high, pure sound produced by placing a finger on a string very lightly before plucking or bowing.

Harmon mute A **wah-wah mute** for brass instruments.

Hemiola A rhythmic device in which two groups of three beats (*strong-weak-weak, strong-weak-weak*) are performed as three groups of two (*strong-weak, strong-weak, strong-weak*).

Heptatonic A 7-note scale: see p85.

Heterophony, heterophonic Simultaneous performance of a melody and a variation of the melody. In jazz this is often when one player improvises on the melody while another plays it straight.

Hexatonic A 6-note scale: see p85.

Homophony, homophonic A musical texture in which all parts (melody and accompaniment) move in similar rhythm creating a chordal effect.

Hook A repeated, catchy **motif** in jazz and pop music.

Interval The distance between two pitches: count the letter names between the notes including the first and last, so C to G is a 5th. See also **compound interval**.

Inversion (of a chord) A chord is inverted when a note other than the root is in the bass (e.g. chord V). In first inversion the 3rd is in the bass (Vb); in second inversion the 5th is in the bass (Vc). The chord of the dominant 7th can be written in third inversion (V⁷d).

Inversion (of a melody) When the intervals in a melody stay the same, but the pitch moves in the opposite direction, e.g. ascends instead of descending. The result is akin to a mirror image of the melodic **contour**.

Inverted pedal See the explanation for **Pedal note**; an inverted pedal note sounds higher than the harmonies beneath it, instead of lower.

Italian 6th An augmented chord containing the root, major 3rd and augmented 6th.

Kumbengo An ostinato pattern in kora playing.

Latigo Spanish for 'whip', a type of glissando in tango music. It is played fast, ascending or descending, to mimic the sound of a whip (as used by Argentine gauchos).

Latin rhythm Music of South America and Cuba is characterised by syncopated rhythms and beats of unequal length, e.g. 3+3+2.

Legato Played smoothly, without breaks between the notes.

Leitmotif A recurring fragment of music that represents a specific character, event or emotion.

Looping A technique in electroacoustic music and sound production in which a short passage of sound material (the loop) is repeated to create **ostinato** patterns. Loops can

be created in many ways, including sampler, synthesiser, sequencer, drum machine, and computer.

Marcato Marked, or accented playing.

Melisma A series of melodic notes sung to the same syllable.

Mickey-mousing A technique in film music of synchronising the accompanying music directly to action on screen. The term is derived from early Walt Disney films.

Middle 8 The central, contrasting section of a song, in pop and jazz music, also called the bridge, or B section in an AABA song form. Often, but not always, 8 bars long.

Milonga A type of tango dance.

Mixolydian Major scale with a flattened 7th.

Mode, modal, modality An alternative series of scales to the diatonic major and minor scales, often used in traditional music.

Modulation The process of changing key midway through a piece.

Monophony, monophonic Music consisting of a single unaccompanied melody line.

Mordent A melodic ornament.

Motif, motivic A short, distinctive musical idea: see also **leitmotif**.

Motor rhythm An insistently repeating short rhythmic pattern that conveys an almost mechanical, unstoppable quality, a typical example being two semiquavers plus a quaver.

Mute Device attached to an instrument to soften the tone and produce a different timbre, for string and brass instruments; see **con sordino.**

Neapolitan chord Major chord based on the lowered supertonic (second note) of the scale. Most commonly it appears in a minor key and in first inversion, when it becomes a **Neapolitan 6th**, so in the key of E minor, this is a chord of F major in first inversion. Romantic period composers first began to use it in root position, then preface it with its own **secondary dominant 7th**, and then explore using it in a major key. The chord usually resolves to the dominant.

Neapolitan key The key found a semitone higher than the tonic key.

Nonatonic A 9-note scale: see p85.

Non-functional harmony Harmony where the chord progressions do not follow the needs (functions) of standard harmony: **see functional harmony**. In non-functional harmony chords are used for their inherent 'colour' rather than for their customary progressive function.

Non-harmony note A note outside of the harmony with which it is sounding, so usually dissonant.

Note of anticipation A non-harmony note which is approached by step from the note before, and then stays the same as the harmony changes for the following melodic note: essentially it is a note from the next chord played early.

Nuevo tango Modern style of tango music, introducing new instruments such as saxophone and electric guitar; strongly associated with Astor Piazzolla.

Octatonic An 8-note scale: see p86.

Open-5th chord A chord containing only the root and 5th, with the 3rd missing. See also **bare 5ths** and **power chord**.

Ostinato A rhythmic, melodic or harmonic pattern repeated many times in succession (similar to a riff in pop music).

Panning In music technology, altering the left and right distribution of the sound.

Parallel 3rds A texture where a melodic line is simultaneously played (doubled) a 3rd higher or lower, thus creating a consonant richness.

Parallel harmony The parallel movement of two or more lines often producing chords with an identical intervallic structure.

Passing note A non-harmony note placed between and connecting two harmony notes, each of which are usually a 3rd apart. Passing notes are usually unaccented (on the half beat, or second and fourth quarter beats), but can be accented (on the beat, with no accent symbol required).

Pedal note A sustained or regularly repeated note, usually heard in the bass, while the harmony above changes between various chords. Usually the pedal note is the tonic or dominant.

Pentatonic scale A scale of only five notes. The most well-known is formed by the black notes of the piano (C♯, E♭, F♯, G♯, B♭) and is anhemitonic, meaning that there are no semitones included (only tones and minor 3rds); alternatively, the pentatonic scale of C, E, F, G, B is hemitonic, as it has a semitone between E and F.

Periodic phrasing Music, typically of the Classical period, in which the melodic phrase is structured in pairs of 2-bar mini-phrases making pairs of 4-bar phrases, making pairs of longer 8-bar phrases, and then 16-bar phrases, and so on.

Phrygian mode Minor key with a flattened second note, a scale with a dark character.

Pitch-bend A short slide up or down to the main note.

Pizzicato An instruction for string players to pluck the string instead of using the bow.

Polarised Texture common in Baroque music where high-pitched instruments are accompanied by a bass continuo, without instruments included in the middle range. More recently, polarised texture is often used in film music as it portrays an expansiveness (e.g. for a landscape scene) and allows dialogue to be clearly heard spoken in mid-register.

Polyphony, polyphonic A musical texture where two or more parts move independently of one another.

Popular song form A common structure in songs in music theatre and popular music, in which there are four phrases where the first, second and fourth are related to give a pattern of AABA: see also **32-bar song form**.

Portamento A performing technique of sliding from one pitch to another, often associated with singing: see **glissando**.

Power chord In pop and rock music, a chord that consists of the root and the 5th, especially on electric guitars and often used with distortion: see **open 5th chord**.

Primary triads Chords I, IV and V in any key, so called because they are of a primary importance in establishing the tonality of a composition.

Push rhythm A rhythm that anticipates the beat, often entering a quaver earlier than expected, and sometimes tied to the first note of the bar to heighten the effect.

Raga A scale pattern or melodic motif used as the basis for melodic improvisation in Indian classical music.

Recitative A type of vocal music where the words are the important element, and are usually sung in free time and in normal speech rhythm.

Relative major/minor A pair of keys which share the same key signature, one major and one minor: for example, the relative minor of F major is D minor, and the relative major of D minor is F major.

Resolution The release of tension in music as the harmony moves from a discord to a concord, or point of tonal stability.

Reverb An electronically-produced echo.

Riff In jazz, pop and rock, a short, catchy melodic or rhythmic idea repeated throughout a song.

Rip In jazz, a quick upwards glissando to a note.

Ripieno In Baroque music, this is the ensemble who play the tutti sections, in contrast to the soloists.

Ritenuto Immediately slowing down.

Ritornello The main structural form for concerto movements in the late Baroque era. The term is also used to name the orchestral section heard at the opening and returns in various keys throughout a movement, punctuated by vocal solos (**episodes**). The ritornello may be repeated whole, or in part, or with variations.

Rondo A musical structure popular in the Classical period in which a main melody alternates with a contrasting section (ABACA).

Root position A triad with its fundamental note in the bass line.

Rubato An interpretative performance technique, often associated with Romantic music, where some nuanced flexibility of rhythm is used (both holding back and pushing on) to create expressive affect.

Scale Eight notes, making up all the notes in a key. The degrees of the scale have the following names:

- I   Tonic
- II   Supertonic (i.e. above the tonic)
- IIII   Mediant (i.e. halfway to the dominant)
- IV   Subdominant (i.e. the 5th below the tonic)
- V   Dominant (i.e. the most dominant overtone to the tonic)
- VI   Submediant (i.e. halfway to the subdominant when descending)
- VII   Leading note (i.e. leading to the tonic)
- VIII   Tonic

Secondary dominant 7th A dominant triad which resolves to a chord that is not the tonic, often the dominant of the dominant, V^7 of V.

Secondary triad Chords ii, iii, vi and sometimes vii in any key, i.e. excluding those which are primary chords.

Sequence (in melody) The immediate repetition of a **motif** or phrase in the same instrumental or vocal part but at a different pitch.

Simple time A metre in which the main beat can be subdivided into two. The opposite of **Compound time**.

Simultaneous quodlibet A composition combining several different pre-existing melodies all heard at the same time, often light-hearted in manner.

Smear In jazz, a loud, possibly coarse, slide away from a note.

Sonata form The most common structure for the first movement (and sometimes other movements) of compositions in the Classical style, comprising exposition, development and recapitulation.

Sotto voce Meaning literally 'under the voice', an indication that a hushed or whispered performance is required.

Source music In a film, music which is played on instruments seen in the film, such as a string quartet at a wedding.

Staccato Short, detached playing, with gaps between the notes.

Stop time In jazz, a rhythm where some beats are not played, e.g. 1 2 (rest) 4, 1 2 (rest) 4.

Substitution chord A complex chord which functions in the same way as the simple chord it replaces.

Sul ponticello Direction to a string player to bow very close to the bridge, producing a whistling tone.

Sul tasto Direction to a string player to bow or pluck the strings over the fingerboard, producing a gentler tone.

Sus4 chord Major or minor chord where the 3rd is omitted and replaced with a 4th, creating an open sound without the 3rd and a dissonance between the 4th and 5th.

Suspension A note from a previous chord is carried over to the following chord, creating dissonance, before resolving. There are four categories: three are understood in terms of the interval above the bass (4–3, 7–6, 9–8), and the fourth is where the suspended note is in the bass.

Swing In jazz and blues style, the first quaver of a pair will often be played slightly longer than the second one.

Syllabic Vocal music in which each syllable of the lyrics is sung to a single note: see also **melisma**.

Sympathetic strings Also called resonance strings, these are auxiliary strings on an instrument which vibrate when the main strings are being played, providing a halo of sound around the note that is being played.

Syncopation The effect created when accented notes are sounded off the beat or on weak beats.

Tala Rhythmic patterns used in Indian music.

Tambor In tango, a form of pizzicato that causes the string to rebound off your finger creating an unpitched drum-like sound.

Tenuto From the Italian 'to hold', this direction indicates the player should hold a note slightly longer than written, often for emphasis.

Ternary form A musical structure of three sections with similar outer sections and a contrasting central one (ABA). Usually the B section is in a contrasting key to the A sections. Can also be described as arch form.

Tessitura The average range of an instrumental, or more usually a vocal, piece. It is worthy of remark if a piece is written high or low in the range of the instrument or voice performing it.

Through-composed A song where each verse is set to contrasting music.

Tierce de Picardie A major tonic chord used to end a piece of music in a minor key.

Tihai In Indian music, the repetition of a polyrhythmic phrase three times, often to round off an improvisation or a whole piece.

Tonal The use of standard major and minor keys. Not all music is tonal: see also **modal** and **atonal.**

Tremolando A musical effect created by the rapid repetition of a single note, usually associated with string instruments.

Triad, triadic A melody based on the notes of the triad: the root, 3rd and 5th above it. A triad can be major, minor, diminished or augmented.

Trill An ornament: a fast oscillation with the note above or below the given note.

GLOSSARY

Tritone An interval of an augmented 4th (or diminished 5th), so called because an alternative way of counting it is as an interval of three tones. It so happens that this is exactly half an octave.

Tritone substitution Common in jazz, a chord where a dominant 7th chord is replaced by another dominant 7th chord whose root is a tritone away.

Turn A melodic ornament.

Underscore Music that is played under dialogue in a film score.

Unison Two or more people performing the same note or melody; in a choir when everyone is singing the same melody, even though the men are singing an octave lower than the women.

Verse-chorus form Simple song form common in pop music, alternating verses and chorus which contrast with one another.

Vibrato A performing technique where the pitch of a note slightly wavers to give the sound greater warmth and resonance.

Wah-wah mute An effect when a brass player alternately applies and removes a mute; on an electric guitar when the player controls output from the amplifier with a pedal.

Walking bass Common in both Baroque music and 20th century jazz and blues, a bass part with a regular rhythm throughout a piece, akin to feet walking.

Whole-tone scale A scale where there is a whole tone between all the notes, with no semitones as there would be in a conventional scale.

Word painting Music written to reflect the meaning of the words, e.g. ascending when the words mention climbing a mountain.

Acknowledgements:

Instant Crush
Words and music by Thomas Bangalter, Guy-Manuel de Homem-Christo and Julian Casablancas. © Copyright 2013 Imagem Music BV. Imagem Music /Julian Casablancas. All Rights Reserved. International Copyright Secured.

Agony (From 'Into The Woods')
Words and music by Stephen Sondheim. © Copyright 1987 Rilting Music Incorporated. Print Rights Administered by Hal Leonard LLC. All Rights Reserved. International Copyright Secured.